MANAGING DIFFICULT ENDINGS IN PSYCHOTHERAPY

United Kingdom Council for Psychotherapy Series

Recent titles in the UKCP Series
(for a full listing, please visit www.karnacbooks.com)

MANAGING DIFFICULT ENDINGS IN PSYCHOTHERAPY
It's Time

Lesley Murdin

Series Consultants

Aaron Balick
Alexandra Chalfont
Steve Johnson
Martin Pollecoff
Heward Wilkinson

LONDON AND NEW YORK

First published 2015 by Karnac Books Ltd.

Published 2018 by Routledge
2 Park Square, Milton Park, Abingdon, Oxon OX14 4RN
711 Third Avenue, New York, NY 10017, USA

Routledge is an imprint of the Taylor & Francis Group, an informa business

Copyright © 2015 by Lesley Murdin

British Library Cataloguing in Publication Data

A C.I.P. for this book is available from the British Library

ISBN-13: 9781782200512 (pbk)

Typeset by Password Publishing, Burnham Deepdale, Norfolk UK

CONTENTS

ACKNOWLEDGEMENTS

I owe thanks to all my patients and supervisees who, as always, teach me very well. I would like to thank Meg Errington for her wisdom and encouragement. I also offer my thanks to all the members of the Foundation for Psychotherapy and Counselling who have generously helped me in writing this book. In particular I would like to thank:

Deirdre Schueppert, Lalage Lee, Peter Ball, Wendy Monticelli, Rosie Claxton, Caroline Pirquet and Christine Scrivener.

For his generous help with preparing the MS and unfailing support and encouragement, I would like to thank my husband, Paul Murdin.

ABOUT THE AUTHOR

Lesley Murdin practises as a psychoanalytic psychotherapist. She teaches and supervises in many contexts and has considerable experience in running psychotherapy organisations. She has worked for the registering bodies UKCP and BPC, chairing committees over many years. She was CEO and National Director of WPF Therapy and has been Chair of the psychoanalytic section of the Foundation for Psychotherapy and Counselling. She has published numerous books and papers.

UKCP SERIES PREFACE

Alexandra Chalfont
Chair, UKCP Book Editorial Board
Philippa Weitz
Commissioning Editor, UKCP Book Editorial Board

The UK Council for Psychotherapy (UKCP), holds the national register of psychotherapists, psychotherapists qualified to work with children and young people, and psychotherapeutic counsellors; listing those practitioner members who meet exacting standards and training requirements.

As part of its commitment to the protection of the public, UKCP works to improve access to psychological therapies, to support and disseminate research, and to improve standards, and also deals with complaints against organisational as well as individual members.

Founded in the 1980s, UKCP produces publications and runs meetings and conferences to inform and consult on issues of concern to practitioners and to support continuing professional development.

Within this context, the UKCP book series was conceived to provide a resource for practitioners, with research, theory, and practice issues of the psychotherapy profession at the heart of its aims. As we develop the series, we aim to publish more books addressing issues of interest to allied professionals and the public, alongside more specialist themes.

We are both extremely proud to be associated with this series, working with the UKCP Book Editorial Board to provide publications that reflect the aims of the UKCP and the interests of its members.

INTRODUCTION

I wrote an earlier book, *How Much is Enough?* (Murdin, 1999), which looks at the reasons why therapy can go on for too long and offers thoughts on coming to a timely and successful conclusion. This book is about endings that come to difficult conclusions, endings that cause pain to the therapist as well as to patients. The book focuses on the nature of the difficulties encountered by therapists in ending clinical work and in ending their own work altogether, through illness or through retirement.

What makes an ending difficult?

Ending is painful. That statement immediately conjures up contradictions and voices expressing all the contrary possibilities: ending, they say, may be a success, a triumph, a relief. Through my own experience of bereavement, I am well aware of the complexity of the experience of loss in the life of an individual, as well as in clinical work.

Julian Barnes' memoir on death, *Nothing to be Frightened of*, was published in 2008. (Barnes, 2008) It is a rich, personal conversation about death and dying, loss, and our attempts to protect ourselves from the impact of our knowledge of the certainty of death. We are not used to much certainty in our ordinary lives and the inevitability of death is disturbing to most people, both because it is an ending and because it is certain. Benjamin Franklin pointed out, "In this world nothing can be said to be certain, except death and taxes." (Franklin, 1817) Franklin was conveying a message about the inevitability of taxes but, as Barnes points out, most people fear the very inevitability of death, their own and that of those they love. This must relate to the sense of helplessness that we have all experienced as a young infant and have struggled to leave behind in our growth to adulthood. Barnes discusses his own and his brother's attitude to death which, as for most people, involves a consideration of the promises of the great world religions that something of us will continue after death. He discusses with his brother, who is a philosopher, reasons for believing or not believing in an afterlife,.In general, his own point of view is that death is the end for all of us and anyway, not many concepts of heaven would be pleasing to him for all eternity.

Barnes is able to discuss the thoughts of his own death with equanimity. The type of relationship he had with his mother made her death something he could accept. His father's death became a more painful loss as time went by. He began later to see the pathos of his father's last months of life. He describes the process, after a visit to his parents, of leaving his father at the door "hunched" over his walking frame and his mother hurrying out to the car to ask whether he thought his father had deteriorated. His mother blamed his father for falling and for his panic when he had fallen, and she was unable to pick him up. She seemed to want her son to become the other parent discussing the father as though he were their child. She was in the process of losing her partner and seeking to make her son into her new one.

If we cannot find a satisfactory defence against the pain of loss and ending, the only constructive possibility is to find a way to live with it. Psychological therapy puts itself forward as one way through which people can learn to live with loss. Ending gives the therapist the opportunity to try to understand the way in which the patient approaches loss and his attempted denials of the pain that could be brought to the surface.

This book is about the difficulty of ending, but it is also about the learning that we can draw from the endings we know have gone wrong, as well as those that have worked well. We must also consider an ending that therapists often find very difficult too: their own retirement. We are aware that some endings have been left too late, so that the therapist has died while still working. Of course, any of us might succumb to illness or an accident at any time and this cannot be helped. Nevertheless, over the age of eighty, the likelihood of illness, disability, and death itself increases dramatically every year and therapists must take this factor into account.

Continuing to work saves the therapist from the pain and distress of putting an end to therapeutic relationships. But if the therapist dies, patients are left distressed and, at the same time, they no longer have their own therapist to help work through their distress.

One of the reasons for writing this book is that I have sat on ethics committees and complaints panels for several organisations. I have come across many causes for complaints, but one that stands out is the effect of unresolved conflict over painful endings. This is hardly surprising as psychotherapy is about human suffering and ways of enabling people to suffer less. Since ending is part of universal human experience, we need not be surprised that it presents itself as part of the matter that needs to be addressed in the therapeutic process. The professions of counselling, psychotherapy and psychoanalysis have not yet paid enough attention to the problems of bringing our work to a conclusion. Ending is part of a new mental and emotional structure that can be at least moderately satisfactory for both parties. I am hoping this book will help therapists to live well through a difficult time.

Language

I use the term "therapist" to include "psychoanalyst", "psychotherapist", and "counsellor". I am mainly speaking from my own background in analytic theory but I believe strongly that we have much in common across the modalities. Above all, we each put the wellbeing of patients first. I am aware that practitioners in other modalities will have different views and different methodologies, but because we have a great deal in common we should be able to learn from each other's writing.

For the people who come to see us, the term "patient", meaning "the one who suffers", seems preferable to me, and I use it instead of "client" which meant *dependent* in its original form.

Except for particular named individuals, I use feminine pronouns for the therapist throughout. For clarity, I then use the masculine pronoun for the patient.

Confidentiality

None of the illustrative vignettes that I have used refer to actual people, although they are drawn from my experience.

CHAPTER ONE

Ending causes pain

What harm can ending do?

What harm can arise from a poorly managed ending? Not only is useful work missed but the work that has been done may be spoiled. This is determined, to some extent, by the length of the therapy that is ending and by the strength of the attachment that has developed. The attachment, of course, need not be positive. In fact, the negative and ambivalent relationships that arise can lead to emotional disturbance which is by no means healed by ending the relationship. Some patients who are angry may want to walk away rather than stay and face the fear of being angry with the person who seems to hold the promise of something better for the future. This patient fears that he will destroy his own hope.

William Blake's poem "The Poison Tree" conveys the common belief that anger will be fatal. He grows a metaphorical poisonous fruit which kills his enemy:

I was angry with my friend:
I told my wrath, my wrath did end.
I was angry with my foe:
I told it not, my wrath did grow.
In the morning glad I see
My foe outstretched beneath a tree.

—Blake, 1794

One of the achievements of psychotherapy might be to enable the expression of hostile and negative feelings without the fear that they will be deadly. The alternative might be to expect that other people will be delighted with the honesty of the person who has become able to express feelings. This person might then be hurt to discover that the expression of anger often leads to an angry response, and is certainly not always welcomed. Both of these reactions may be experienced and made less dangerous in the therapeutic process.

In his book, Julian Barnes writes of his mother, who was an atheist. She said "People only believe in religion because they are afraid of death". (Barnes, 2008, p. 8) Barnes says that this is a statement that shows his mother's confidence in her own views. Nevertheless it makes an interesting point. Most people are afraid of final endings and in particular of death, whether their own or that of someone they love. Religions that offer a life after death have attractions in the context of this fear. The practising psychotherapist has to help people deal with loss in whatever way they can, and maybe help them discover how to return to a trusting state of mind that enables the individual to begin to live in the present.

Freud wrote the paper "On Transience", (Freud, 1916) in which he conducts a debate with an imaginary poet. The poet argues that the knowledge that all we are, have and see must come to an end and reduces the value of life—therefore we must believe in life after death. Freud argues that transience and our knowledge of endings add to the value of that which must go. This of course has relevance for therapy because, whether it is time-limited or open ended, it will still have an ending which must be recognised. Transience value is scarcity value in time. (Freud, 1916, p. 305)

The therapist may share with the patient the fear of the losses that an ending brings. This may be one of the reasons why endings can go wrong. This book will consider some of these possibilities. On the other hand, how could we expect therapists to be without this fear? Should we in fact wish for that? If the therapist were immune from this aspect of the human condition, she might be able to help patients to end their therapy without a tremor of regret, but that would perhaps not help the patient to deal with the grief and distress that normally accompanies bereavement. The fear of death is a curious phenomenon for psychoanalysis because, as Freud pointed out, (Freud, 1915, p.296) the unconscious cannot entertain the idea of death. We also know that consciously, we all find it difficult to imagine our own death and total absence from the world.

Ending as transition

Ending psychoanalytic work can be difficult, not only because all ending is seen as symbolic of death, but also because it indicates the ending of at least one stage of a process of development. Since most people have been exposed to at least one of the world's religions, most have formed views about death as the end or as a transition to another state of being. The approach to ending may carry with it this ambivalence about whether it is an ending. Ending therapy is usually a transition and carries its own particular shades of doubt and uncertainty. The therapist handing the duty of care back to the patient has to accept that she is no longer needed. One useful way of thinking about the function of the therapist is in relation to Donald Winnicott's concept of the transitional object. (Winnicott, 2011, p. 107) The infant finds an object, often a piece of soft cloth, which feels to him to be partly himself and partly Other. It allays anxiety and is often essential for going to sleep. Its use is to enable the infant to negotiate the stage of recognising the existence of external objects that are not under his control, and then gradually the limits of his own body and mind. The fate of the object is to be gradually "relegated to limbo", that is to say, it is not forgotten but loses its meaning as the transitional area extends to the whole cultural experience of the individual.

Endings that are destructive

The therapist is experienced in something of the same way, until she can be allowed to lose meaning and is no longer needed to allay anxiety because the patient has achieved his own understanding of inside and out. For a time, however, the therapist is seen in phantasy as part of the patient herself and is not allowed to diverge too far from being what the patient wants her to be. This is the phenomenon described by Heinz Kohut as the twinship transference. In *Analysis of the Self*, (Kohut, 1971) Kohut describes the functioning of the narcissistic transference, which by definition is a form of mirroring. The patient is highly anxious and seeks to lower the level of anxiety by unconsciously coercing the other to be like the self. This produces the twinship transference in which the analyst must be perceived to be the same as the self and any deviation or expression of her individuality is fiercely resisted. The commitment to this idealisation is related to the demands of the grandiose self of the toddler. Jacques Lacan elaborates the ego's mistaken sense of its own perfection in early childhood in *Le Stade du Miroir Comme Formateur de la Fonction du Je*. (Lacan, 1949). From then on, each of us sees the world through a distorting prism.

Termination may be difficult just because, in Winnicott's model of simply growing out of a stage, the process seems to lack drama. Of course this ending, that is simply a letting go, might be less painful. Perhaps the pain is needed to enable the process to be useful for bearing bereavements. An alternative view of ending which recognises the more violent, frightening aspects of endings comes, for example, in the poem by Robert Frost in which he describes the way the world will end in fire or ice. He knows that desire can burn and destroy but has to consider that ice can also destroy. Even though fire might be the more likely way in which we destroy each other, we now know that the universe will die in coldness and darkness: "To say that for destruction ice/Is also great/And would suffice". (Frost, 1955)

This of course is metaphorical, but it reminds us that we imagine ending as destructive. There are many different ways of imagining the ending of the therapeutic work, including T.S. Eliot's thought in "The Hollow Men" about the way the world ends, "not with a bang but a whimper". (Eliot, 1936) One useful quest for the therapist is to elicit the patient's image of ending and death in order to discover whether he can live with it.

If a whimper is what is expected and is the predominant image, both the therapist and the patient may expect, and then experience, some disappointment. This is clearly conveyed by Kohut in his paper, "The two analyses of Mr Z". The patient ended his first analysis in a calm way but without much feeling:

> What was wrong at that time is much harder to describe than what seemed to be right. Yet, I believe that, although both the patient and I must have known it precociously, we failed to acknowledge and confront a crucial feature of the termination phase. What was wrong was, to state it bluntly, that the whole terminal phase, in stark contrast to the striking contents that we transacted, was, with the exception of one area, emotionally shallow and unexciting – noteworthy because the patient was not an obsessional personality, was not inclined to split ideation and affectivity. On the contrary, he had always been able to experience and to express strong emotions. He had always experienced shame and rage with great intensity and often felt deeply upset about setbacks and wounds to his self-esteem; and he could also react with a warm glow of triumphant satisfaction when accomplishment and success enhanced his self-esteem. To draw specific comparisons: nothing in the terminal phase – neither his experiences in real life nor his experiences in the analytic sessions came anywhere near equalling the emotional depth with which in earlier phases of the analysis he had talked about his idealization of the pre-Oedipal mother and his admiration for the counsellor. Only the feelings concerning the parting from the analyst appeared to have real depth; and his ultimate acceptance of the fact of having to give up the analytic relationship seemed hard-earned and genuine. (Kohut, 1979, p. 12)

Kohut was unable to make much of this, although in fact the two parted "with a warm handshake". Mr Z then returned for a second period of analysis when they were able to understand something of what had been missing. He had a dream of his father appearing outside the door with a pile of colourfully wrapped presents:

> ... [H]e was in a house, at the inner side of a door which was a crack open. Outside was the father, loaded with gift-wrapped packages,

wanting to enter. The patient was intensely frightened and attempted to close the door in order to keep the father out. (Kohut, 1979, p. 8)

At first this dream was taken in a warning sense: "beware of Greeks bearing gifts". But, in the second analysis, Kohut was able to help the patient reach the understanding that his father might bring him gifts that he would want and need. The second analysis allowed the primitive mirroring transference, arising from the grandiose self of the young child, to develop into a much more realistic view of the potential in the father and the danger of idealising the mother. Not many therapists have the opportunity for this sort of revision of their understanding. Most often, the thinking must be done immediately, using the learning that we can derive from experience, both our own and that of others.

The end of the story

The account of Mr Z illustrates that one of the pains of ending is the missed opportunity. When you say goodbye to a person, job or place to live, you close down all the possibilities for the future that might have been. Therapists tend to like stories. That is one essential qualification for the job, and while it helps us to be able to listen with interest to the stories of patients, it makes ending difficult. Freud described the process of analysis as being like sitting on a train while a passenger describes the scene that passes across his vision outside the window. (Freud, 1913, p. 134) If the listener cannot see what is outside, he needs the seeing passenger to tell him. No wonder the listener feels some resistance to letting his companion leave. Daniel Spence, in his discussion of therapy as narrative, took up this image:

> Not only is the patient not merely reporting what is seen through the window (the mind's eye), but he or she may also have the fantasy that the analyst knows what the patient knows and that, as a result, the patient's private language needs no explanation. (Spence, 2003, p. 879)

Spence pointed out that the passenger is by no means an objective observer who merely reports what he sees. There is a continuous choice, selecting details or points of emphasis; there are also effects arising from the context. Above all, the speaker is aware of the listener and will alter the associations because of it. He invokes the patient's tendency to use metonymy – substituting the part for the whole, for example, "the crown" for "the monarchy". This may be done to protect the listener or the speaker, but will be used along with many other techniques to hide and blur the edges of the message that needs to be conveyed. Sometimes the patient speaks elliptically because he believes that the therapist knows what he is thinking. This assumption involves a level of magical thinking that is difficult to disentangle. It takes time and requires what Winnicott saw as gradual disillusionment. (Winnicott, 2011, p. 111)

Another part of the distortion of the account of the landscape may come from the difficulty of seeing. The landscape may be dark, or the country may be concealed at crucial moments, for example by a train on another line, or more seriously by camouflage imposed by others. The patient might be short sighted and unable to see very far or very clearly. He may be unaware of his own deficiency if he has never been able to see more. The therapist may begin only after time to understand what the limits are. Freud's image can be extended to describe the distortions that arise from processes of projection or transference.

Digging up the past

The second image of the therapeutic process that Spence considers is Freud's archaeological metaphor. The therapist is engaged in piecing together a story from a number of fragments that are, perhaps, dug up in the wrong order or puzzlingly broken and fragmented. Whether or not the therapist now thinks that she is embarking on some process of reconstruction, she is confronted with fragments and is trying to make some sense of them for both herself and her patient. An ending will leave her with fragments that have not been satisfactorily labelled or assigned a place. The archaeological metaphor, however, does allow that the pieces of the past may be mysterious but they are still available to be examined. The train window analogy implies that the view from the window, once passed, has gone forever and there is no second chance. Both of these images hold some truths for the therapeutic process. The moment when a patient tells the therapist of some event from the past will never return in exactly the same way. Some aspect of the context will change and, if the therapy comes to an end, the listener will be a different person. Maybe the patient will have to listen to himself. Since we know that memories are constructed through many elements that co-exist at the moment of retrieval, we have to accept that the memory, and all that it tells us, may be different each time and may be gone forever when it has once been told.

Loftus and Bernstein (Loftus & Bernstein, 2002) have shown the extent to which memory is variable. They argue that experiments have shown that memories are distorted in a way that makes it impossible for the therapist to distinguish true memories from false. In some ways this research is disturbing but it is also exciting. The truth that looks clear and historical one day becomes blurred and indistinct or may be completely changed the next. The effect is that, however much archaeological digging the therapist may help the patient to achieve, there will still be a sense in which the major achievement of the therapy will be to enable both people to accept that there are few certainties and that what is clear today may need a new approach tomorrow. Living with this degree of uncertainty is always going to demand courage and the ability to find, and live through, inner resources.

So far, this chapter has considered the pain of loss that the therapist might feel in accepting the patient's wishing to end. The patient might feel some of the same kinds of disappointment or frustration, but he will also have his own disappointments. The extent to which the therapist has become a transitional object will determine to some extent the potential for separation either with maturity or with great pain. In the process of development, the good enough mother allows her infant to have the illusion that the breast is part of him and under his magical control. Maturity involves the gradual loss of the need for this belief. Winnicott (Winnicott, 2011) says that it can be left behind as the capacity to relate to another outside the self develops. He also adds that the creativity that this stage shows can be developed in the arts: in music, in painting, and in writing. One way or another, a transitional object can be allowed to become itself and be separate.

Winnicott himself recognised that his formulation was provisional. It leaves out the importance of dependence which can grow into mature interdependence. This is important because the therapeutic relationship might develop beyond the point when the patient requires the therapist to be part of himself without separate thoughts or wishes. When the patient can move on, he can allow the therapist to be separate. If this can be achieved, it brings into existence the possibility of the sadness of losing the separate person whom the therapist has become. This makes clear some of the reasons why patients might end therapy too soon. There is a growing awareness of the importance of the relationship as the therapist becomes a separate person. Better to leave before the attachment grows greater and the sadness of leaving becomes more intense. The patient may also have an intellectual understanding that he will have to leave at some point, and may feel ashamed of the long term dependency that he sees himself beginning to feel. Of course there are many possible reasons for ending therapy unilaterally, and this kind of fear might remain unconscious or dimly felt, but unacknowledged.

Angry endings

The angry ending is known to most therapists and may be a defence against the experience of sadness. Inexperienced therapists take the anger at face value, but they might perhaps think that there is something beneath stormy accusations of inadequacy and incompetence. That is not to say that these are not also important. All therapists should consider what they have done or not done, and how much they have failed to live up to what might have been expected of them. Whatever can be understood of the angry patient, the aftermath is painful for both patient and therapist. The patient has to take away an image of a damaged and demolished therapist who may never have had the chance to convey her own point of view, or show that she can survive.

This is the sort of experience that can lead to levels of guilt that may even be conscious. We know that guilt can eat away at the individual, especially if it echoes guilt from a previous experience. The guilt might or might not be justified, but it can sap confidence and lead to a depression that is difficult to shake in the future. At its most extreme, the belief that the therapist has been destroyed will take on something in common with a sense of having committed murder.

Shakespeare's Macbeth suffers all sorts of ill effects from guilt, both conscious and unconscious. He suffers from flashbacks and delusions, but he also cannot sleep:

> Methought I heard a voice cry, "Sleep no more!..."
> ....
> Sleep that knits up the ravelled sleeve of care
> The death of each day's life, sore labour's bath,
> Balm of hurt minds, great nature's second course,
> Chief nourisher in life's feast.
> (*Macbeth*, Act II, scene ii, lines 35-40)

Macbeth, as we know, was driven to a sort of madness by guilt over his own ambition. He had killed the king who symbolised his father. In fact, Lady Macbeth found that she could not go beyond this image: "Had he not resembled my father as he slept, I had done't". (Act II, scene ii, lines 12-13) For both Macbeth and Lady Macbeth, the sense of having destroyed a parent is devastating and makes it impossible to continue with ordinary life. No-one is suggesting that leaving a therapist has any conscious connection to murder, but it may have a connection to deeply buried guilt and anxiety.

Mélanie Klein, following Freud, would perhaps agree that we all have deeply buried feelings of guilt over emptying the mother's breast or the bottle, leaving it useless and in fantasy, destroyed. The infant begins to be able to withstand these anxieties by means of good experiences which can be stored in a kind of central reservoir of trust and good faith, which Klein called "the good object". (Klein, 1975, p. 67) In order to maximise the benefit of these experiences, time is needed. What Klein discovered clinically and emotionally in this area has been confirmed by the neuroscientists of the twentieth century through more rigorous observation. Pathways of stimulation and response develop in the neurons in the brain and new information tends to go along these well-worn paths. The possibility of making new paths is still there in adulthood. That is why time is needed for repeated experiences with a therapist who is not destroyed and does not return in macabre form, as Banquo's ghost memorably did, at least to Macbeth himself, even if no-one else could see him. The ghost was, in itself, an accusation of the crime which Macbeth had committed in having him murdered: "with twenty trenched gashes on his head, the least a death to nature". (Act III, scene iv, lines 26-27)

The therapist is known to be alive and well if the ending is allowed to take place with appropriate reflection, thought, and awareness. The patient then has to deal with his own anger in knowing that the therapist can manage well enough without him. Patients will show this as anxiety through questions that hint at wanting to know how the space will be used. How soon will the patient be replaced and how totally will his absence be forgotten? We see both of these conflicting desires in many adolescents who want to be allowed to leave home freely and with parental blessings, and yet also want to be missed and have a place to return to whenever he or she wishes to do so.

The therapist has to leave

Patients feel sadness when therapists choose or are forced to leave their work. This is a cause of ending which will be examined in more detail in this book. If a therapist retires, she will usually give appropriate warning to her patients and enable them to express their feelings about it, both their sadness and their anger. There is likely to be more difficulty when the therapist loses a job because of reductions in therapy services. Local authorities and medical services are likely to take decisions to reduce psychological services from time to time, and this sometimes means that patients are not given enough notice. This is partly because the nature of the work is not understood by officials. Patients are bewildered and may not know whom to blame but will be deeply hurt by the therapist, who seems either unable or unwilling to avert the fate that is threatened.

Therapists are forced to give up their work for various external reasons, but one that is particularly difficult for many is the passing of time. Therapists grow old like everyone else, but if they are not employed by an agency like the National Health Service, or a charity with its own rules, no-one except friends or supervisors can say, "It's time you retired". Possibly, therefore, therapists try to defend themselves against recognition of the inevitability of aging and death by continuing to work. Work may be brought to an end by illness, death or some recognition of incompetence that cannot be hidden. Patients have suffered greatly from therapists with progressive illnesses who were unwilling to say they would stop before they were forced to do so by weakness or symptoms that could no longer be disguised. Patients who know that their therapist is ill may struggle with the knowledge, conscious or otherwise, that work may be keeping the therapist alive, and therefore they cannot take themselves away. This may mean that not only is the patient not finding the help that he needs, but his burden is increased by the therapist in the role of patient.

This book will therefore address the question of retirement, what helps therapists to begin the process, and how it moves forward. For this, it will be important to hear the voices of therapists themselves, as well as to address the relevant theory. One of the important sections of the book will therefore consider all the losses that are involved in the therapist putting an end to her own clinical career and moving into a new phase of her own life, just as her patients will have to do.

Sometimes the therapist is able to help her patients through recognising the mixture of feelings that are evoked. Sometimes, however, an inexperienced therapist will so wish to make clear that the ending is not her free choice or her fault that she might prevent the full recognition of the value of her own agency and, at times, her own courage in setting about the process. Both of these could help the patient to recognise and deal with his own response. If there is an external person or agency causing the ending, the therapist may wish to avoid being seen as this cause. The effect of the therapist saying "it is not my fault, they are making me do it" is to put her on the same level as the patient. This sets up a sibling position in the Oedipal structure. The family situation that is echoed will consist of a sibling who reports the decisions of the parents but cannot change them. She is seen as helpless in the context of these powerful but probably unseen and unknown parents. This may still be useful if the resentment engendered can be recognised and seen as a pattern of relating for others the level of reality can be recognised, as well as the element of the pattern that is derived from the past.

Freud saw the importance of power that is demonstrated in the anxiety many people feel about ending. (Freud, 1915, p. 297) If the fear of death is equivalent to the fear of loss of power, then one of the difficulties for the therapist when she is faced with the pain of loss will be in enabling the patient to manage his own feeling of helplessness. This fear will lead to a risk of aggressive behaviour as the patient seeks to reassure himself of his own power and control. This would be a fairly clear and understandable reaction. Sometimes this fear is difficult to identify and analyse because the fear of helplessness is masked from the patient himself by appearing as fear of dependence or commitment. Instead of showing aggression, the patient may appear unmoved and casual, able to take it or leave it and apparently, coming down on the side of leaving it.

The patient decides to leave

Patients who feel that they need to leave the therapeutic relationship may bring all sorts of reasons which will be difficult for the therapist to dismiss or counter. Not liking some aspect of the therapist's technique or behaviour is difficult to state, and even if it is stated, may be difficult for the therapist to take seriously. The main reason may be presented as shortage of money or time or material. The pain of loss may be completely subsumed into other sorts of shortage, and the therapist may have her attention deflected into trying to find ways of solving these problems. She may try to change the time or offer a lower fee. This may even have the temporary effect of resolving some of the questions the patient might have about the level of the therapist's commitment, but it may not be enough to alter the fundamental problem, which can remain untouched.

Sometimes patients leave therapy because it is an exercise of power that comes only, or mainly, from the intensity of that relationship. This is particularly true of therapists in training. The patient may know that his continued attendance is important to a candidate, and may know that leaving might hurt the therapist in many ways. Usually the knowledge of this power is sufficient, but in some cases it will be exercised, particularly if the therapist has not managed to get to the heart of the transference scenario that is being recreated. Research on premature termination carried out by Cooper et al. (Cooper, E., Hamilton, M., Gangure, D., & Roose, P., 2004) showed that premature termination is a relatively common experience for candidate analysts. In their study of 163 patients accepted as training patients, nearly one-third terminated prematurely.

Defences against the pain of loss

As in every aspect of our lives, we are all able to avoid some kinds of pain in endings while we succumb to others. The understanding of the pain of loss leads us to consider the ways in which defences themselves increase suffering. The patient who defends against impotence by perverted sexuality, or the patient who defends against isolation by obsessive pursuit of love from the therapist, may cause severe disruption to therapeutic work and distress for both people.

This book will therefore consider the complaints that have arisen from patients who felt that they were not considered enough by their therapist, and the distress of the therapist who is suffering from the effect of the pain of the patient. Complaints have shown that ending is difficult and that therapists do not always pay enough attention to helping the patient to end. Sometimes there is no way the therapist could help more than she has, but sometimes the disturbance caused by the patient's defences leads the therapist to behave in uncharacteristic ways.

Complaints are important and need to be heard for the sake of the patient. Complaints that are not upheld can still seriously damage a therapist's confidence. Nevertheless, complaints are unusual and should not lead to defensive practice, although the learning from them must be taken into account. Such learning is very painful for the therapist caught up in a formal complaint, but it is ultimately valuable for her and for her colleagues if they pay attention to the possibility of making mistakes. The main theme of complaint in relation to endings is the therapist's refusal to accept the patient's decision. This refusal has been shown by the therapist who insists that the patient should pay for sessions missed after the patient had announced his decision to leave. Other therapists have refused to see the patient after she has decided that therapy is no longer useful or tolerable from her point of view. If the patient has no opportunity to express his pain over the ending, this may be thought to be grounds for complaint.

Ending tests every aspect of the therapeutic relationship, especially when the experience is negative. Codes of Ethics demand that the emphasis must always be on the wellbeing of the patient, and on the ability of the therapist to help him accept the inevitability of endings culminating in death for all who live. Doing this without becoming clinically depressed is a challenge for all human beings. Depression, in the sense of the poignancy of loss, is inevitable but it frightens people. In our culture, there is now more awareness of the dangers of moderate or severe depression. Lord Richard Layard, in his report of 2000 on depression, showed that debilitating depression is widespread in the population and difficult to change. What is necessary is public awareness that sadness, and even periods of low mood, are normal phenomena from which we recover naturally. The kind of severe depression that responds to chemical intervention is a different thing altogether.

Facing and accepting sadness is not easy for either the patient or the therapist. Ending a long established therapeutic relationship brings various outcomes. Not only will the therapist no longer have an effect on the patient's life, she will not know any more of the story. This hunger for the next development might sometimes lie behind the practice of some therapists to book follow-up sessions. This practice certainly changes the nature of the ending, and may help uncertain patients make a definite ending date. Unfortunately, the ability to decide to end may have developed because of the change from an ending to a temporary absence, and may not help with the essential problem. The only hope here is for the therapist to be clear that there is an ending, and any follow-up is just to check how the ending is working out for the patient.

CHAPTER TWO

Time in psychotherapy

Time rules human life, and in fact all life on Earth, which blossoms and dies. We all experience mutability, once seen as the fate of everything beneath the Moon. As we now know, everything in the Universe changes. Small wonder that the consulting room is a place where time matters. The pain of loss discussed in the previous chapter is made inevitable by the passing of time. As Angela Molnos pointed out in *A Question of Time*, (Molnos, 1995) the pace of modern life is much faster than it is has ever been. This is a cliché now but it seems obvious that the Internet and high speed broadband must have made a difference to our expectations of instant gratification, and have come to symbolise our wish for speed. Not only do we demand that our pleasures are immediately available, but we expect all services to be at our command. The UK Government, at the time of writing, is fighting a continuing battle to reduce waiting lists for health services such as treatment for cancer. Apart from such known risks, the person who is suddenly taken ill may be lying on a trolley at an Accident and Emergency service because no doctor is available, and this can be a matter of life and death. Although we are all in a sense waiting for death, we do not accept that death should be hastened for some unfortunate people because the necessary services were not available quickly enough. The assumption is that we should not have to wait.

Enduring waiting

Waiting has become unacceptable and yet it is an essential component of analytic work. Because we do not know at the outset how much time will be needed, the therapist and the patient both have to accept that it will be necessary to wait and see. Some patients welcome the slow, timelessness of the analytic session. At least the space between the beginning and the end of the hour has its own pace, but it is for many people the only time when there is no immediate goal. If the patient cannot see a clock, there is no awareness of the passage of time in our ordinary train-catching sense. Patients sometimes appreciate this reflective space and feel the value of waiting to see what occurs to them, although often in the early stages, people plan what they are going to talk about in order to keep away the terror of infinite time and infinite empty space which silence might bring.

Time is a purely relational concept. There can be no time unless there are two points which can be placed in relation to each other. It is one of the four dimensions recognised by modern science, although there is some doubt about how to define its existence, apart from the psychological construct recognised by the human brain. It is certainly a human construct, and as such we have to teach children to understand it. Children usually learn concepts of the future before they acquire any concept of the past. The motivation for learning what is meant by "tomorrow" or "soon" is clearly strong. What happened yesterday is no longer so important unless it relates to a promise. A small child might find it worthwhile to remember that "you said I could" and how long ago that was. Ill treatment in the past belongs to a different category of events which can become present again in the consulting room.

This brings us back to time in the consulting room, which is both outside ordinary time, and is open to being thrust into earlier times that are still living in some way. Molnos (Molnos, 1995, p. 6-7) points to the difference between the modern western concept of time as an arrow, and the mediaeval concept of time as a cycle within a universe enclosed within a crystalline sphere. The images lack subtlety but they do show something of the emotional colouring of each period. The flight of an arrow is irreversible and swift. If you miss what is happening, it is gone forever. We are all made well aware that a great deal is happening all the time and we hear echoes of world, national and local events as the backdrop to our personal events. All this passes each day, and what we have not caught and held in some way may have gone forever.

T.S. Eliot has expressed, in his "Four quartets" (1944), the way in which footsteps echo in the mind. Time past and time future become possible only in the present moment, which is a kind of pivot on which all our memories and hopes and fears are poised. His four poems represent the four elements, and perhaps show in themselves a cycle in which the end is present in the beginning and the beginning returns at the end. Mankind may bear reality better when it is given the aesthetically pleasing shape of this cycle or circle. By this stage in his life, Eliot was taking an overtly religious position, and when he spoke of fire, it was the fire of purgation. For him, the end is not the end but man must suffer before reaching the possibility of immortality.

Can the present alter the past?

However attractive we might find the whole concept of a cycle in which we return to a maker and do not die, the concept of human development is based on the linear view of time. Freud emphasised the concept of *nachträglichkeit*, which has been translated in various ways. As "deferred action" it implies that the past is still effective in the present, and much psychoanalytic work demonstrates that this is in fact the case. On the other hand, if we take it in the preferred sense of retrospective action, the present can affect the way the past is viewed. This is a different way of thinking about the work of analysis but it is also very important. Patients in analysis will point out that nothing that can be said in the session will alter the terrible truths of the past as they perceive them. On the other hand, the theory of *nachträglichkeit* enables the therapist to know that the work of the sessions can give the past a different meaning in the present. This is inherent in the work of the therapeutic couple. Andrew Samuels wrote that the ability of the patient to think about parental intercourse with equanimity is a sign that he or she might be ready to end. (Samuels, 1989) It is a way of saying that generosity and gratitude can now be more available and can triumph, some of the time, over resentment, guilt and envy. It makes development into a more circular concept in which the developmental stages are in some sense reworked through the experiences of the present.

Sergit Barzilai writes that Freud himself never formulated a definitive theory of *nachträglichkeit*, but even in an early letter to Wilhelm Fliess in 1896, he writes of the process by which "later events rearrange the original material". (Barzilai, 1997) Memory traces may be given new meaning as a result of maturation, or of specific situations in the present. As Laplanche and Pontalis (Laplanche & Pontalis, 1967, p. 112) observe:

> Psycho-analysis is often rebuked for its alleged reduction of all human actions and desires to the level of the infantile past... In actuality, as Freud has pointed out, from the beginning the subject revises past events at a later date (*nachträglich*), and it is this revision which invests them with significance.

Relating the past to the present in this way makes a cyclical theory of time more useful to the psychotherapist than a purely linear theory. Events in the past have not disappeared but will still affect the present and may be seen again, even though they may be different in their reappearance. Since the present will inevitably affect the way the past appears, the connection between past and present can be seen as a circle. This applies both to personal and private events, and to the world view that each one of us holds.

Our picture of the Universe that we inhabit is constantly changing and developing. The current world view is not optimistic, although it is on such a scale that most individuals do not often think of it as relevant to their own personal concerns. The idea of a cyclic universe that would expand and contract forever is no longer accepted by cosmologists.The recent ideas in the early twenty-first century are that the universe is expanding more and more rapidly, which means that eventually everything will be infinitely far from everything else. This of course is on a time-scale that we cannot conceive, and therefore we do not need to concern ourselves with it. This is true, but it gives a background to our life, revealing the mortality of our planet, and our Sun which we might find depressing. This is added to the knowledge that we all have of the inevitability of our personal death.

Some but not all of our patients come to us with this as part of their cultural background. There is no need for any particular knowledge of the physics involved for an individual to have the idea that the process of creation and development leads to an ending rather than to an open and continuing path. One of the tests of depression might be the ways in which a person can allow his own life to have meaning for him, in spite of the knowledge that everything we can see and know will come to an end. This knowledge could be used to put a black line under any work that can be done, and can be used to destroy and damage ordinary human optimism and hope. On the other hand, it could be accepted and set aside so that the personal work that each individual does is allowed to have meaning and worth. In this context, the time in the consulting room needs to be time out from a depressed and hopeless view of the world.

Time in the session

One of the main opportunities for the therapist to work with the difficulty of time as a persecutor is at the beginning of each session. The patient returns after some time away and has to reassert the possibility of dialogue with the therapist, who has become a stranger in the meantime. Some people can manage the absence and go straight back to a connection at the beginning of the session, but others take many repetitions before they can re-engage without too much fear or hostility.

> Olive was beginning therapy with Mrs F. She came because she had experienced sexual abuse from an uncle and her experience with a dominating boss at work had brought it back to her consciousness. She arrived at the beginning of sessions and sat in silence. Her thera-

pist, Mrs F, was disturbed by this silence. She allowed ten to fifteen minutes but by that time she had begun to worry about whether she should help the patient to begin. She tried saying something about how difficult it might be to trust a stranger and to launch into talking without knowing what response she would get. This seemed to help and for two weeks, Olive came in and began to talk after just a few minutes. Then the painful initial silence began to lengthen again. She talked about the problems she had with her teenage daughter and this enabled Mrs F to understand her own anxiety better. She was worried about speaking as intrusion and not speaking as neglect. Both of these elements in the adults around her had distressed Olive. Her mother had never seemed to notice that things were not right with her, and her Uncle had intruded unforgivably on the young twelve year old girl. Once she understood this, Mrs F was able to begin thinking about the dilemma that confronted both her and Olive with her own daughter. She could then go on beyond the immediate dilemma to consider how absence and separation made these difficulties more prominent.

It would be difficult to establish that the separation makes these problems worse if we did not have the evidence that the problem shows itself at the beginning of the session. After twenty minutes or so of talking, the patient apparently began to feel more able to trust her therapist and to feel less endangered by the new meeting.

Another situation in which the separation of patient and therapist causes pain is shown by Laura:

Laura was a woman of sixty-five who was consulting a therapist because of her depression linked to her husband's diagnosis with an inoperable brain tumour. The therapist had to cancel a session for personal reasons, and Laura was reasonable and understanding. She even said that it would be quite a relief not to have to come as she had a dentist appointment on the same day. Her therapist did not entirely accept the cheerful assurance that it did not matter. She decided to wait and see what Laura would disclose . The next session after the missed one was very informative. Laura said that she had been very upset and was reminded of being sent back to boarding school by her mother, who never seemed to understand what the parting might mean. She said that it was absolutely forbidden to cry. This was both for her mother's sake, and because the other children would tease any child unmercifully if he or she were found to be crying. Nevertheless, she knew the pain of separation was great and that what hurt most was the uncertainty that the mother understood or cared about the parting. Mrs F was then able to see the importance of the action that she had taken, and was able to understand the importance that she had already acquired for the patient.

For both of these patients, the consulting room was the theatre, as we might expect, in which the past was acted out and the time became the past in the present.

Time for a patient like Laura was both too fast and too slow. The time before the parting went too fast. There are many different ways in which the time hastens a loss or a parting.

Elizabeth was a woman of forty-three. She had ended a relationship with a married man who had said for many months that he would prefer to be with Elizabeth, but she had accepted that he was not going to move and at last simply said to him, "Do you want to live with me or with her?" His answer prevaricated again and she walked away sadly. She found herself unable to settle with what had happened and had gradually become more depressed. In the sessions, she said that she believed that it was too late for her to find a new relationship and too late to have children. Her love and her body were useless to her or to anyone else. The sessions seemed to the therapist to pass slowly and with a deadly depressed weight. The patient spoke of time rushing by and bringing her no hope. The therapist had the difficult task of helping Elizabeth to find some pleasure in her own life, and to enable her to become someone who would be less of a burden to whoever she was with. This was easier thought than achieved. Elizabeth was an academic and often wanted the sessions to turn into a philosophical argument about the value of life. The therapist found this very tempting and enjoyed the intellectual level of the debate. Yet she had to understand that this was not fruitful. Elizabeth wanted to stay in her own medium so that she would be able to continue to believe that there was no hope for her.

At one point, both therapist and patient began to feel that there was no way out other than suicide. The patient spoke about death as the relief from her constant struggle with despair. The therapist had to acknowledge that at times the picture looked bleak. Yet she knew that she had to avoid being sucked into the same state of despair as the patient. In this case, an ending was visible to both but it was an ending to be avoided as long as there could be hope. The therapist sometimes found her mind empty of all thoughts other than the need to hurry up and find a way of enabling this woman to find her life worth living. The consoling answer to this might be that the therapist is not able to do this, and therefore should not expend her own emotional energy on trying to do it. Instead she needs to work at the still daunting task of helping Elizabeth to find the reasons for her inability to imagine a future.

This brings up the question of desire. The paradox is that Elizabeth fears that she can desire only what she knows she can never have. So she suffers from having, on the one hand, a passionate and deeply felt desire and, on the other, an inability to desire anything else. This is the central core of depression. One question will be whether she can overcome her narcissistic sense of entitlement enough to accept what she has, and mourn what she does not have. More important than this though is the ability to tolerate uncertainty. Elizabeth frequently makes statements that show that she believes that she is particularly unlucky, and will never have the good fortune to meet someone with whom she can enjoy having a relationship.

Jacques Lacan defined desire as the relationship to a lack. (Lacan, 1964) Desire is forward looking by definition as the lack is felt in the present, but it has a history and a predicted trajectory into the future. Desire is about the memory of satisfaction achieved in the past on which fantasised satisfaction for the future is based. The infant has experienced some sort of satisfaction from feeding or from being cleaned and erotic pleasure from being touched, unless the carer was deliberately cruel or psychotic. These experiences may have been short-lived and may have vanished as soon as the child was old enough to be left to his own devices. Searching for paradise lost is one of the main activities of patients in analytic therapies. Recognising this quest for what it is can help people to live more satisfactorily with what they have in the present.

The difficulty of living in the present

Ironically, the trouble for patients who find time rushing by too quickly, as well as for those for whom time passes slowly, is in a way the same. Neither can savour the present moment. Learning to do so some of the time is one of the best uses that can be made of the analytic hour. Because it will not be shortened or lengthened but will stay reliably the same, the patient can learn to use the present moment. The emphasis on free association shows the patient that the therapist values what is happening in the present, in spite of its apparent irrelevance or triviality. This is a clear desire on the part of the therapist for the patient's present to be captured and maybe spoken aloud. This would be a first step to enabling the patient to find his own desire as opposed to the desire of others, such as a parent or a teacher. The route, however, is still beset with the difference between the patient's own desire and that of the therapist. This is one of the areas where the decisions to be made about ending (see Chapter Seven) need to be examined to see what they show about the inhabiting of desire.

If the therapist understands the patient's need to discover the meaning of his own desire before he is ready to leave, the meaning of time in the consulting room will have to change. The point at which time does not fly straight forward but can allow the past into the room has to give way to ordinary clock time, in which we have agreed that there will be x many hours or weeks or months left and then we will part. At this stage, there is still scope for the patient to bring his own illusional or delusional time into the room:

> Patrick agreed with his therapist, Mr D, that he would leave on a date three months ahead. He was about to begin a new training which required that he should see a therapist with a specific training. Both he and his therapist were angry that his current therapist was not considered appropriate for him to continue. After some delay, he decided that he did wish to pursue the training and that he would have to accept the rules. They both agreed that he would end in four weeks. Mr D was angry but thought that he should try to conduct the ending in a way which would be helpful. He was also stung by the rejection and wanted to show that he could work well. He tried to connect the material that he was hearing with the

ending. Patrick rejected it. He too was angry, but he was angry with Mr D for not being good enough. Mr D did not see that the interpretation needed was that Patrick was ashamed of him as he might have been by a parent who turned up at school dressed, perhaps, in a way that was embarrassing. As a result, Patrick seemed uninterested in all the interventions that Mr D made on the subject of his anger or his sadness about the ending. His anger remained beneath the surface and his silence continued unremittingly. Mr D was too defensive of himself to understand the nature of the anger. The last day came and Mr D felt thoroughly unhappy and disgusted with himself. He was ashamed and knew that he had in fact not worked well, even though he had consciously thought that he wanted to. Patrick said, "Well, thanks for everything" and left.

This is an example of a countertransference difficulty which the therapist is unable to resolve for himself. Possibly a supervisor could have seen what was going on, and could have unravelled the transference a little. As it was, both the therapist and the patient lost the opportunity for discovering something more of the way in which the past was still present in the room, and were unable to change to the present in time for the ending.

The therapist's time shrinks

Therapists have to manage the curtailment of time in other ways. One of the most distressing is when illness makes it impossible for the work to continue. There are times when there is no choice and the therapist is clearly unable to continue. Her time must then dominate and the patient has no choice but to recognise that he must end. Human frailty is distressing but can be accepted if the therapist is still able to work with the patient's experience, which may be anger as much as sympathy. The therapist in this situation will have an ambivalent relationship with the passing of time. If she has an illness from which she expects to recover, she will be happy for the time to pass quickly. If, on the other hand, she has no expectation of recovery or improvement, she will find it very difficult to hear her patients' cries of need. She might well expect, or at least hope, for sympathy if she tells the truth. Telling the truth will be fraught with difficulty.

It may seem too much of an intrusion to allow patients to know, for example, about a diagnosis of progressive multiple sclerosis. The therapist in this situation will have to imagine the humiliation of the gradual failure in control and independence, and will not easily allow her patients to imagine the same. This might be partly out of concern for them, but is also partly about the difficulty of giving up the position of being in control and becoming the vulnerable one.

For the therapist in this position, time may become a persecutor. The first problem will be to decide what, when and how she will tell her patients. This sort of plan is best made in conjunction with a senior and experienced member of the profession. Each patient may need to have consideration given to their own experiences before a decision can be made about what is helpful for him or her. The therapist, however, makes a decision about what to do and when to do it, but may find that she does not tell every patient in the session in which she planned to do so: something gets in the way. Most often the patient comes to the session with some major change or problem of his own. The therapist makes this an excuse to herself to leave it till the next session. Once she has allowed herself one delay, the next one will be a little easier and the week may end with much of the work still to do. She will gradually begin to feel that there is not enough time and that she has to rush into something for which she is not yet ready.

The problem of the future in the present

This last problem is that of the future in the present. The therapist mentioned above is preoccupied with what she imagines the future to be. This of course is well known to all of us, including our patients, and is responsible for some of Elizabeth's suffering. However desirable a state of not knowing might be, we all suffer from our fantasies of what might be coming, and this shapes our present and so of course shapes the future in the direction that we have envisaged. We have the phrase "a self-fulfilling prophecy" to describe the extent to which a person can influence his own future by his beliefs about it.

Several forms of mental distress are caused by the failure to accept the unknowable quality of the future. Depression is one state which has much theory now about its nature and origin. We know that the depressed person has no way of believing that the future could be better than the present. He is actually convinced that it will be worse. He has no desire in fact. The therapist has great difficulty in arriving at any dialogue about his wishes for the future because no wishes or desires can be formulated. Freud expresses the connection of depression to the past and to the losses of the past in his famous paper "Mourning and melancholia", written in 1915. (Freud, 1917) It also breaks new ground with the idea that the depressed person suffers from alienation of desire. The person's own desire has been overshadowed by the lost person who has died. This element from the past has strayed into the present and is affecting both present and future. While this is operating, there is little hope of a satisfactory ending.

Recognising the power of the past may cause as many problems as it solves. The patient quite rightly may say, "I had a terrible time as a child but It happened and what can you do to change It?" The answer to this of course has to be "Nothing". The patient then gets angry with the therapist, who is seen as useless and exploitative, taking money for no good reason. This anger may turn into a reworking of the past in which the therapist is the bad and heartless one, so that the patient can be sure that he did not cause the ill treatment and harm himself. Somehow the blame scenario must be left behind because it will lead to a painful and useless ending if it is not understood and used to bring relief from the torment of this reminiscence. Closely linked to this is the re-enactment of the bad times from the past in the hope that each time it may turn out to be different. It can turn out to be different this time only if the therapist can recognise what is happening and put it into words.

Patients who ignore the past

A different approach to the past is taken by the patient who focuses on the present and refuses to allow the past to have any meaning for him. These people insist that their problem is in the present and their childhood has nothing to do with it. They have no interest in the time dimension and wish to be treated purely in terms of a problem to be solved. The therapist has the task of helping them to see other possibilities, and to allow their rigid beliefs to be challenged. This patient is taking a view which might relate to that of Jacques Lacan (Lacan, 1964), who did not envisage a gradual change over linear time as the aim of analytic treatment, but rather saw changes as discrete shifts from one structure to another. His understanding of *après coup*, the French translation of Freud's term *nachträglichkeit*, is that the person historicises the past by his current way of historicising the past in the present. This implies that the point for the therapist is not to discover facts about the past which are in any case unknowable, but to discover what the patient makes of the past. If he makes of it a story which is irrelevant to his present, that says something powerful about his isolation. He is not, as Isaac Newton acknowledged himself to be, "standing on the shoulders of giants". (Turnbull, 1959, p. 416)

Lacan (Lacan, 1964) considered that the unconscious is structured like a language, and therefore the working of the unconscious will echo the ways in which time is embedded in language. English has a fairly complex system to show the tense of an action. Sometimes this changes. For example, the tense difference between "may" and "might" is increasingly misunderstood, and it looks as though the language will lose this distinction altogether in the future. Some languages do not use inflection to denote tenses. In fact, English has no future tense in this sense and has to use periphrastic constructions to indicate the future. Angela Molnos points out that the Hopi Indian language does not express tense or aspect in any way. (Molnos, 1995, p. 6) She also points out that there are cultural differences in the attitude to waiting and to punctuality which may show themselves in lateness or simply not attending. These differences cannot be automatically interpreted but have to be understood in relation to the person's background. The Sioux Indian language has no word for "late" and therefore has no way of thinking about what social relations might require in terms of punctuality. A Nigerian patient was frequently late for her sessions, and it was not until a supervisor pointed out that this might relate to the fact that she had not been in this country long that the therapist was able to address the point.

The therapist needed to say that the end time was not moveable and therefore the beginning time needed to be unmoveable also. The cultural differences needed to be addressed as well, although this may be difficult because they are often unknown to one or both people.

There are psychological reasons for lateness which vary from person to person. In general, we could consider that most of them will fall under the heading of unconscious questions of control. The therapist clearly controls the end of the session by saying "It's time" or using whatever form of words she has acquired, probably passed on from her own therapist. Some patients attack this sign of parental authority by delaying their compliance or simply ignoring what the therapist has said. Others may comply without question, leaving promptly and without fuss. They may then transfer the battle ground to the beginning of the session. However self-destructive it may be, the patient can choose to come late to the session, just as he might choose to come on time. The session may begin on time, in the sense that the therapist is there and waiting, probably thinking about him and the reasons for his lateness. The patient may deny in his own mind that the session begins until he is actually present in the room. He may feel that he can take control over a dominating father or mother who ruled over the child's time by refusing to allow the therapist to have her way and begin on the hour. The therapist's job is to disentangle the transference and discover who is being controlled by the lateness, so that the pleasure derived from denying her is conscious and is attached to the person to whom it belongs. The patient can then begin to think about it rather than simply endlessly repeating the pattern.

> Maria came to see Mr T because she had a very difficult relationship with an alcoholic mother and was worried that she might not be a good enough mother to her own baby, which was due in five months. She said that she was tired and found it hard to get up. Mr T was dubious but felt that he did not know enough about being pregnant to argue with her. She came ten to fifteen minutes late to every session. She said she was sorry, but she was always late for everything and it did not mean anything in particular about the therapy or the therapist. When Mr T thought about what she was doing, he understood that she was seeking to punish the mother

and that his role in the transference was as the self indulgent mother who could not be relied upon for any help, but who made arbitrary and cruel demands on her daughter. Maria was required at home to put her mother to bed every evening and could never enjoy time with friends her own age. She was expected to be at home, watching her mother get drunk, and was beaten mercilessly if she ever chose to disobey. Although her mother had died some years before, there were many strands of guilt to be disentangled before a clear strand of anger emerged, which was just visible in the daughter's wish to absent herself.

Sue Kegerreis sees the time boundaries of the session as an expression of the Oedipal struggles of the patient with the father. (Kegerreis, 2013) Time is part of the law established by the father, and to defy it is to defy the law of the world which the father represents. Refusing to accept the law that enables society to function with appointments and all sorts of expectations of the responsibilities of ourselves and others will have various kinds of impact on the therapist. She may feel the narcissistic injury from the patient who does not wish to spend the whole session with her. She may be relieved that she does not have to worry about promptness with this particular patient, who can be relied upon to be late. Some therapists find themselves coming late too, or bringing a book to the session to read while waiting. Of course, the particular shades of the countertransference that she experiences must be used to understand the kind of projection that the patient is using.

Time and the therapeutic hour are highly relevant to the matter of ending and leaving. Each therapist's own attitude to the frame will show itself to the patient, and will enter into his feelings about how she will manage the final ending. Lacan wanted to avoid the tyranny that he thought the fifty minute hour exercised (Hill, 2002, p. 185) and he developed various rationales for ending at a point of emotional intensity. People remember discontinuity and unanswered questions much more than smooth continuity and finished conversations. (Ibid., p. 189) Nevertheless, Lacan substituted his own tyranny and his patients had to deal with the authoritarian father who was able to make things begin and end according to his thinking. The ending of the session is a kind of punctuation, and punctuation, as we know, can make a great difference to meaning. An exclamation mark makes a sentence like, "You are doing very well!" mean something quite different from the same words with a question mark. Lacan's arguments were also based on the arbitrary nature of the fifty minute hour, and the way in which it cuts off the speech of the patient. The therapist's obsessional neurosis might seem to encourage that in her patient. Patients delay their revelations because it might be getting too near the end of the session and there will not be enough time.

Even when the therapist is following a completely predictable path through to the end of the fifty minutes, patients have very individual responses to the therapist's words at the end of the session. Everyone is familiar with the patient who looks at his watch and is prepared for the end of each session. Others only guess when it is time but avoid entering anything that they want to discuss near the end. Conversely, the most important but difficult revelation may suddenly appear just as the person is leaving. Here, the therapist's use of the firm frame may be a defence for the patient. One of the technical questions for the therapist becomes whether or not to bring it back at the beginning of the next session. Most people would leave the patient to return to it, but the question is whether such a revelation should be allowed to be forgotten.

One other aspect of Lacan's view of time is his description of the human construction of temporality. (Lacan, 1964, p. 143) Each process involves three stages which are linear, not constructed according to clock time but are intersubjective and develop through the tensions of expectation and waiting. He saw time as marking stages in perception leading towards a conclusion: the moment for seeing, the time for understanding, and the time for concluding.

Allowing for these processes involves something like Freud's concept of working through a psychological process, and cannot be addressed in a given hour in a given way. The whole analytic process for an individual can be seen to follow this trajectory but how long it will take for any given person is of course unpredictable.

Each person's anger over the ending of a session or of the therapist's term before she goes on holiday can reveal something of the process that he is trying to complete. In mourning, the patient, like the rest of the world, may hold on to his grief in order to hold on to the loved person who has died. In the same way, the anger with the therapist may be needed in order for the patient to have the time for the understanding to develop.

> A patient, Ruth, was seeing a therapist, Mr J. She described her difficult relationship with her elderly mother who never seemed pleased to see her, and yet complained bitterly whenever Ruth said she had to leave to go home. Mr J was held up by traffic one morning on his way to his consulting room and was ten minutes late. He suggested that they might add five minutes to the end of the session if that suited her. She said that was all right and spent the rest of the session in angry silence. Mr J said, at the next session, that he thought she had agreed in the same spirit in which she continued to visit her mother, in other words a need to placate the one making demands. She said that yes, perhaps it did feel a bit the same. He went on to elaborate a little, adding that his offer of extra time had in fact felt to her like a demand, and put him in the role of making demands on her just as her mother did. She burst into tears and said that it was all too much and she could not manage any of it any more. "It's all your fault", she added hopelessly and then "No, it isn't, but I can blame you now, can't I?"

Ruth's reaction demonstrates the importance of time boundaries to the patient, and illustrates the problem for the therapist who has to miss a session or lose some time. Substituting other time or more time is not going to feel all right. Agreeing to it puts the patient in the position of the one who is letting you get away with something. This demonstrates the difficulty of negotiating an ending which, for a patient with unresolved mourning, will feel like letting you get away while the anger and guilt has not yet been addressed. The impetus in this sort of situation will be to walk out so that you recognise that harm has been done. Like suicide though, this ending will not achieve its aim as the patient will not be there to know the effect of his action.

Time in this focus is a gift, and gifts bring love and hate, guilt, gratitude, and envy. All the most powerful emotions are bound up with the time that we regularly spend with patients. At some level in their minds is the belief that the time we spend is a gift, even though it is paid for and it brings with it the obligations of reciprocity and appreciation. The analyst who understands this will be able to help the patient to untangle the threads of guilt and envy and discover where they lead.

CHAPTER THREE

The patient decides to end

This chapter will consider conscious reasons for patients to choose to end their therapy. Theoretical discussion will focus on negative therapeutic reaction and the difficulty of acknowledging good experience with gratitude. Klein is the obvious writer to consider but there are more recent writers who have considered the more positive range of thoughts and feelings like gratitude and generosity.

The chapter will look at the reasons, both positive and negative, that are given by patients for leaving:

• therapist incompetence

• patient's change of circumstance

• money, place, internal changes

• goals achieved.

When any of these factors is in operation for the patient he may feel that he has to leave, but needs the support of an ethics committee to feel justified in doing so.

Therapist incompetence

All therapists make mistakes. The problem is partly that we often do not know what the most useful course of action will be, and mistakes are visible only in retrospect. I know from my own practice that I can come away from a piece of work wishing that I had said more or less, been more focussed, or got my timing better. Other things I know I do but will not recognise them until afterwards, sometimes long afterwards. Most patients are generous enough to allow me the time to discover my mistake and put it right. I hear similar experiences from the people in supervision too. I also know that the great majority of therapists care profoundly about what they do and seek to improve all the time. Only a few sink into complacency and cease to interrogate themselves and their work.

Nevertheless, sometimes a patient leaves a therapist who seems unable to be what the patient wants or needs. Most therapists will have the experience of seeing a patient who has been to someone else before, but has not stayed for a reason which might sound like incompetent practice.

> Mavis came to see a therapist, Mr P. She described her childhood in which she had parents who were successful bankers and had met in the city of London. Neither wanted to give up their job in order to look after a baby and there was a string of nannies and au pairs. She wished she had been sent to boarding school. "At least I would have been with other neglected children", she added. Near the end of the first session, she admitted she had seen another therapist for a few months, but had left because the therapist kept forgetting things and being late for sessions. Once he had missed a session altogether and did not seem to know that she had waited outside his door for twenty minutes before going away. Eventually Mr P understood that this had felt like being neglected by incompetent parents.

This kind of incompetence can arise from tiredness or illness, or lack of interest in the patient. Sometimes the therapist may recognise that he is behaving in this sort of careless way and seek consultation to discover what the reasons might be. Mr P managed to work out what seemed to have happened for the patient, and he was alerted to the need to be careful of his own organisation and time keeping.

Change of circumstances

Patients leave because their own circumstances change or those of the therapist change to an extent which they cannot tolerate. A therapist's marriage or pregnancy, and the patient's feelings about this, can be one of the most difficult changes to manage. Only the most careful and confident therapist is going to be able to help a patient like Mavis to endure a displacement of this type. The patient will find it very hard to form an attachment to his therapist, and then find that the therapist has an attachment of her own which is clearly more important to her than he is. The pregnant female therapist faces the patient with an emotional demand that could be useful if he can stay and express some of his feelings. This is a situation in which the therapist is likely to be considering ending, or at least taking an extended break. The patient then is confronted not only with a repetition of past losses, but with an actual loss in the present.

The pregnant therapist brings to the mind of the patient the Oedipal dread of a new baby coming to take his place and be more favoured by the mother. Whatever the patient can recognise through his conscious unease, the deeply buried infantile fears are likely to be more accessible at this time. The adult in the patient also wishes to protect the therapist from his hostile wish to destroy the new baby. This state of inner conflict is painful and confusing for the patient, and can lead to premature departure. The desire to protect is often carefully hidden, and the therapist may be more aware of the attack than the motive to protect. She needs to try to bring both to consciousness so that the patient can see the balancing goodness that moderates the hatred and destructiveness.

Money

When a patient is made redundant in their workplace, the resultant loss of income brings the continuation of therapy into question. Here, all therapists have a cultural background partly formed by the organisation with which they trained and partly by their own analysts and supervisors. Some would regard the fee as such a crucial part of the frame that it should be unalterable. Others would put a humane approach first and would offer a reduced fee, at least for a limited period. This may not solve the problem, as the patient will have to endure the humiliation of receiving a charitably low fee. Alternatively, the therapist will be despised as the person who can be persuaded or moved by the patient's need.

If the therapist knows that the patient has a family, especially if there are young children, she will find it very difficult to insist on maintaining her full fee. She will have to balance the need to earn her own living, particularly if the patient occupies one of her early morning or evening slots that are in demand, in contrast with the wish to enable the patient to continue with the work that he has begun. The second part of this balance is the humane concern for the patient's wellbeing, but also relates to the therapist's narcissistic satisfaction in continuing to meet the challenges of a difficult patient.

Goals achieved

This is the most difficult area to assess for both patient and therapist. Fear of not being able to meet his goals may lead a patient to leave precipitately, and may lead the therapist to agree that this is appropriate. Therapist shame and anxiety may be operative and may lead to collusion in a premature ending.

Patients may find their own way to an ending for any of the reasons mentioned so far, but can still feel aggrieved and hurt by the process. As Chair of two different ethics committees, I have discovered that endings that are mismanaged, or are just too difficult for all sorts of reasons, can be the cause of more complaints than any other single factor in the therapeutic relationship.

There are two main areas of difficulty. The first is that people fear that they have become dependent on the therapist, much as they might become dependent on anti-depressant medication. They seek to prove to themselves that they can do without the therapist, but they may find that they have rushed off too soon and the work is only partly done. On the other hand, they might fear the therapist's need for them and flee from an intimacy that has been difficult for them in other relationships. Therapists will need to monitor the possibility of both these kinds of ending, as an ending from each source can be sudden and not allow time for therapeutic input.

The second area of difficulty is related, and arises from the patient's consciousness of his love of the therapist. Freud concentrated on the female patient in his paper "Observations on transference love". (Freud, 1915, p. 159) He found that the female patient shows the therapist what she is like when loving. Considering the female patient with the male analyst, he says that she, "like any other mortal woman", falls in love with her therapist. Patients love in different ways and at different levels, but in order for any work to take place they have to invest some emotional value into the therapeutic relationship. This investment makes it possible for the patient to feel betrayed.

Blum suggests that the early analysts felt betrayed by the loss of Freud himself. (Blum, 1989) He died, as does any mortal man, and his psychoanalysis neither included nor led towards a satisfying theory of ending. However well or poorly we understand our feelings of loss and bereavement, we will still have them. Even without neurotic misery there will always be ordinary human unhappiness. (Breuer and Freud, 1895, p. 305) Freud himself did not see that there would be a final ending to the analytic process for any individual. He wrote "Analysis terminable and interminable" in 1937 as he was ending his own professional life, and his conclusion at that point was that efforts to bring analysis to an end were likely to be premature. On the other hand, he had found that fixing the remaining time for an analysis as being no more than a year had a wonderful effect on his patient known as "The Rat-man". (Freud, 1909d)

Freud did consider the question of what makes a satisfactory ending in analysis. He makes two points. The first is that the analyst considers that the neurosis has been resolved and the symptoms have disappeared. Second, she must be convinced that so much work has been done that the symptoms are unlikely to recur. There is another way of looking at readiness to end, and Freud acknowledges that it is much more difficult to achieve. The analyst must be certain that "no further change would take place in him if his analysis were continued". (Freud, 1937c, p. 376) The nature of the changes would be phenomenological, dynamic, and structural, and would manifest in symptomatic relief and a sense of wellbeing, an understanding of the unconscious conflicts and their derivatives, and improved personality organization and functions. Without formulating it in those terms exactly, many therapists are looking at these criteria, although they would rarely feel able to say that they are "certain". Patients, too, are going through something of this process in their own minds. The difficulty is that maybe the certainty of being ready to make a change is what leads a patient to decide that he cannot risk staying with his therapy because the change is too threatening. Its consequences and ramifications are bound to be unknown.

Blum makes a useful point in that the loss of a significant figure is what makes us all ready to consider how we deal with and process endings. (Blum, 1989) Freud himself left the analytic profession with the same sort of problems as a patient ending his analysis. He is faced with the question of whether he will be able to continue with the development that the therapy has set in train. One aspect of his own thinking will be to consider whether or not the presenting problem has been resolved, or at least improved. Occasionally it will have disappeared altogether from the horizon as the patient has come to understand that other matters are more important and more relevant to leading a satisfying life. Discovering that the problem is not what was originally presented may be a valuable function of the analytic work.

Readiness to end

> A young man came to a therapist to see whether he could escape from the repeated bouts of depression that he had experienced. He thought that he needed to complete one of several projects so that he could believe in his own ability. The therapy enabled him to see that he was always afraid of his father's critical dominance. He found that he could end the therapy, not by being enabled to complete his project, but by being freed from the father who looked at him, whatever he did, with a humiliating gaze.

For this man, the most important aspect of the therapy needed to continue beyond the end of the sessions. Neither he nor his therapist was able to be certain that this would be the case, or that his uncertainty about himself would not return. What was needed was the possibility that he could return to the discoveries that he had made for himself. He would not have been able to do this if everything had depended on the presence of an alternative powerful father, no matter how benevolent. Like the professionals deprived of Freud's presence, he had to come to internalise an object which could continue to help him even after he had left his therapy and his therapist.

In writing to his friend, Wilhelm Fliess, Freud in 1900 had developed a new way of looking at the patient who does not find it easy to reach a negotiated ending, and therefore either leaves suddenly or is unable to leave at all.

> I could have continued the treatment, but I had the feeling that such prolongation is a compromise between illness and health that patients themselves desire, and the physician must therefore not accede to it. (Freud, 1900, p. 409)

Freud appears to be thinking about a negative therapeutic reaction in which the patient is staying as a compromise solution in which he can be better than he was without therapy, but clearly he is not well enough to leave.

It may be in the interests of both the patient and the analyst to prolong therapy on those terms. The analyst may be able to go on hoping that the next session will be better and will bring new insight. She may also have the usual financial and narcissistic reasons for wanting the therapy to continue. Patients have some of the expectable narcissistic reasons for refusing to acknowledge that therapy is not helping as much as they hoped. The patient chose the therapist and committed himself to ongoing work. To admit that the therapy is a failure is possibly inflicting a narcissistic injury on one's self, as well as bringing the end of hope. This aspect of the negative therapeutic reaction will be discussed in Chapter Four.

Perhaps psychoanalysts did not consciously and deliberately deal with termination until they had to confront Freud's demise and their own loss of his reassuring authority. This was a bereavement for the profession, but so were his disputes with Carl Jung and Joseph Adler, among others. Loss would clearly have to be accepted and theorised further. The formulation of the transference neurosis (Freud, 1915) had an enduring impact on all subsequent views of the psychoanalytic process.

The end of analysis coincided with the resolution and genetic re-duction of the transference neurosis, an ideal cure of the ideal ill-ness created by the analytic process. The paradigm of the analytic process neither included nor required a terminal phase (Hurn, 1971). The criteria for termination were phenomenological, dy-namic, and structural, manifest in symptomatic relief and a sense of well-being, an understanding of the unconscious conflicts and their derivatives, and improved personality organization and func-tions, respectively. Freud's topographic and structural aphorisms, "transforming what is unconscious into what is conscious". (1917: 280). *Leistungsfahigkeit*, or productivity, is probably an example of Strachey's tendency to recast Freud's lucid language and pragmatic observations in more scientific/mechanistic terms. Freud's early "experience-close" depiction of analytic goals complemented the metapsychological formulations. His preanalytic comment is still applicable: "much will be gained if we succeed in transforming ... hysterical misery into common unhappiness". (Breuer and Freud, 1895: 305). (Blum, 1989)

Complaints that have been heard by organisations in the UK have shown how powerful the emotions aroused in this last area can be.

Ellen J. was a secondary school teacher. She came from a family in the north east of England. Her father was a builder in a coal mining village. Her mother worked at different jobs, but mostly cleaning. Because her father was not a miner, the family was not seen as a proper part of the village, and so Ellen grew up feeling that she was not really accepted. Children followed her home shouting "Posh girl! posh girl! no one likes you, girl!" She was torn in two because her parents were loving and affectionate, but they were the reason why she was teased or ignored at school. Nevertheless, in spite of, or perhaps because of, her isolation, she did well at school and won a scholarship at 11 to the local grammar school.

At grammar school, she found that she could make a place for herself. The girls came from a wide radius and the internal politics of one village were not well known in the school. Although the girls had the usual sense of hierarchy, with the most attractive and sexy ones at the top, Ellen was allowed her position in the middle rank. At 15, she made friends with a boy from the boys' school at the danc-ing classes that the schools organised together. This would have raised her status anyway, but by that time she had a small group of friends who did not care about her background or her sexiness. They were all academically able and were able to talk about history or Latin without anyone mocking them. She went to a high-status university where her parents were romanticised by the other students who were affecting to believe, or perhaps genuinely believed, in the values of socialism. If anything, she found herself envied by the middle class students whose parents were considered to be uninteresting. Here, after the disjuncture of leaving school, she found another secure home where she could produce the work needed for her course, and could make friends.

Without much thought, she took a job as a teacher in a private school and that was when the trouble began. She was not able to control her classes. She suffered agonies of shame and embarrassment. Her colleagues all seemed to have achieved quiet, well-behaved groups of children. She felt that she was the only one who was not in control. She had met Tom at her university. He was working in the next town and she met him most weekends. He enabled her to feel that she still had some remnants of self-respect, and that the person she had been had not completely disappeared. In her second term, he said to her one Sunday night, as he watched the bus approaching that would take her back to her own flat, "I don't think I can do this any longer."

"What do you mean?"

"I don't think we are really suited. You are too busy worrying about your foul fourth form and you don't pay any attention to me."

Ellen said nothing. She had no breath to speak and her mind was empty. She got on the bus and realised that she was crying. For the first time for many years, she was alone. She was alone with the bullies who would like nothing better than to make her wretched. She had not taken a teaching diploma because it was not required for a job in a private school. She did not know whether it would have helped, but she had thought that maybe a period of teaching practice would have made her more aware of how to deal with those who had no interest in her subject, and needed to be wooed and persuaded to sit quietly and listen. Then she thought that perhaps Tom also needed to be persuaded to wait and listen.

The next weekend she went to join him on Saturday afternoon. She was half afraid that he would not be there, but he was in and seemed to be expecting her as usual. "I don't understand what exactly you mean but I want to try to change, I won't talk about 4 R anymore." She looked at him hopefully but he was impassive, washing a mug, slowly, methodically. "Well, what? Please talk to me."

"That isn't really the point. It's a sign, a symptom maybe that I am not very important to you. I didn't think it would really affect you so I applied for a job in South Africa and I have just heard that I've got it. I shall be leaving in two weeks."

Ellen froze. "You did that without even telling me. You gave me no chance to talk about it? You didn't give me any chance." She found herself furiously angry and almost hit him with the umbrella that she was still holding. He said nothing and picked up another mug to wash. "I'm sorry, Ellen", he muttered. "It's done. I'm going." Ellen lost her anger and crumpled. She wept. He continued to wash his mug and did not come over to comfort her. After a while she stopped crying and stared at his back. "I'll just go then." There was still no reply and she slowly picked up her things and left. Blind with tears, she walked to the bus stop and went back to her solitary room. Everything had changed. The room was more silent and there seemed to be no other place for her.

One strand of Ellen's thoughts as she sat in her chair by the window was that she could not see how she could go back to school on Monday. What had been difficult had become too much of an effort. If one of the children taunted her in some way she would be likely to cry. After repeating this to herself many times she began to add "It doesn't matter" and soon that transformed into "Nothing matters". She had cried most of the way through the night and, although she was sitting two feet away from the telephone, she could not reach out to it to ring the school and let them know that she would not be coming in. Nine o'clock came and went. She sat still.

The effect of not attending was of course difficult. The phone rang. The school secretary left several messages but she sat on.

In the next few days, her junior in the department offered to come and talk to her. She did not pick up the messages but Judith, her friend, came round and barged in. "What on earth is the matter?"

She stopped in concern. "You look terrible. Are you ill?" At last Ellen spoke, telling Judith only "Tom is going to South Africa. He has thrown me away." Judith had not known her for long, but she could tell the seriousness of the reaction. "You need a doctor. Who is he? I'll send for him." In this way, Ellen was visited by a GP who diagnosed severe depression and prescribed anti-depressants. Awakened to her situation at this point, Ellen decided to go and see a therapist.

This story shows how a personal tragedy, usually a loss of some sort, can lead to a reactive depression. More difficult to understand are the forms of depression where we cannot see an obvious loss. In Ellen's case, we might imagine that she would find her way to a therapist. If she does so, there are as many possible outcomes as there are therapists. One story that is possible is an unhappy ending.

Ellen went to see a therapist. The work went well and Ellen found that she trusted Jane and could tell her a great deal about her feelings. This included the way she had experienced her parents, particularly the shame that she had denied so often in relation to her father and mother when she was at school. After about six months, Jane had to take some unexpected time off to visit her mother in the United States, who was diagnosed with cancer. Jane's mother grew more ill and it was clear that she would die within a matter of weeks or months at the most. Jane felt that she had a responsibility to her patients, and she returned to the UK after four weeks. She found an e-mail from Ellen saying that she was no longer confident that the work was useful and she would not be returning for any more therapy.

Jane was shocked and hurt. She felt that she could not bear any more losses. She immediately replied to the e-mail saying that she was sorry to have received the message, but understood that her own absence had been problematic. She added that she thought Ellen was seeing her as if she were the boyfriend who had gone away. Would Ellen come and talk about this? Her session would be kept for her in the following week. This reply gave Ellen the reason she half wanted—to be furiously angry. She did not reply and did not attend the session. Jane wrote her another e-mail expressing disappointment but accepting that Ellen would not be attending any more sessions. She did, however, enclose an invoice for the previous month and, crucially, for the session that was offered but not attended. She wrote that as Ellen had not let her know that she would not attend, she was liable. Ellen was already angry and the invoice seemed to her to be grossly unfair, as indeed it was. She talked to her friend Judith, who joined in the anger and suggested that Ellen should complain to the regulatory body. Ellen put time and effort into discovering how to do this and duly submitted a formal complaint to the appropriate body.

Few people would argue that the therapist in this case acted wisely, but many might see that she had serious problems of her own which accentuated that of her patient, and contributed to her inability to accept her patient's decision. Nevertheless, the welfare of the patient must be paramount, and even though she was going through a very difficult time herself, she had a duty of care. She also had the fundamental justice of the patient's case over payment to consider. Charging for a session which the patient has not agreed to, and has in fact refused as part of a blanket refusal, seems fundamentally unfair.

This is an illustration of gross behaviour which the therapist herself was willing to repudiate when she was asked to consider what she had done. Freud had envisaged two possible endings: there could be a "permanent legal union", presumably marriage, or the "doctor and the patient part and give up the work". (Freud, 1915, p. 160) The third option is that the doctor recognises that it is not the attractiveness of his or her own person that has brought about this state of affairs, but that the patient needs to learn about the resistance that the state of love actually represents. If the patient wanted to impress the object of her love with her willingness to accept the therapist's views, she might appear to be valuing the analyst's interpretations, whereas in fact there is a refusal to pay attention to any analytic work. Moreover, there is the need to be aware of the two risks: on the one hand the patient may play the part of "a woman scorned" and storm off as Ellen did. Alternatively, she can continue to resist all work as not furthering her desire to win the analyst.

Ellen's experience highlights the potential pain of the patient who trusts and comes to love the therapist. Charles Rycroft, following Winnicott, wrote of the dangers of the catastrophic failure of the therapist. (Rycroft, 1955) Freud knew only too well that patients can walk out, as Dora had walked out on him. Even before that his collaborator, Breuer, had ceased working with his patient, Anna O, when she said that he had made her pregnant. Two powerful explosions had taught him caution, but his genius was to see that these explosive endings could have been understood and used to illuminate the reasons for the neurotic misery that each was experiencing.

> The psychoanalyst knows that he is working with highly explosive forces and that he needs to proceed with as much caution and conscientiousness as a chemist. (Freud, 1915, p. 170)

Winnicott took this explosive element in our experience and was able to argue in detail that destructive anger is not only inevitable but that it fulfils a developmental purpose. He argues this in his paper on the use of an object, "Playing and reality" published in 1971,. In this statement of developmental theory, he stated his view that attacking the object is a step on the way to learning that the object is external, and that it is other than the subject.

In the case of Ellen, several things happened that could not be helped. She had suffered a loss of a relationship that echoed her childhood conscious memories of exclusion. She had felt helplessly angry and desperate. Her therapist, Jane, had suffered from the demand expressed in her sick mother's need for her, which would have left her with serious guilt if she had not responded. This much was given, but we can see that it became the arena in which a developmental scenario was played. Ellen was thrown back into feelings that echoed her infancy. She needed to test and find the existence of her own resources and that meant also testing the limits of the other person.

This line of thought would bring us back to the therapist's point of view, which was that Ellen was expressing an unconscious wish to test the therapist and find out whether she would be able or willing to fight for her and bring her back. She certainly wanted to bring Ellen back in order to find out more, as well as to soothe her own feelings of guilt and abandonment. This level of resistance from the therapist may also cause anger and distress in the patient, but can usually be resolved so that it does not lead to complaints. The last straw in this case was the way in which the therapist combined her appropriate professional wish to help the patient get to the bottom of her unconscious wishes, with her own need to have a return for her efforts. Presumably the care that Jane felt for her mother was not acknowledged enough, and her own unconscious wish was to have her work recognised by her patient instead.

This testing may have been somewhere in Ellen's impetuous ending. For Winnicott, the aggressive, even destructive, nature of the attacks against a surviving object serves the purpose of demonstrating that because the object can survive, it is therefore outside the omnipotent control of the subject. (Winnicott, 1971) There is a paradox at the heart of this theory in that the object may be known to survive in some form, but can no longer exist in the form of the therapist if the therapy has to end. Therapists seem to know this at some level, and often resist the ending so that the therapy will continue and the patient could say, "Hello object. I destroyed you. I love you." (Ibid, p. 105) This wish is too much mingled with the therapist's other reasons for wishing the work to continue: narcissistic satisfaction, payment, and professional identity. These sorts of reasons infuriate the patient, who hears the voice of a bully or a narcissistic parent preoccupied with his or her own interest and agenda.

In order to consider the position of the patient who leaves because of a positive attachment to the therapist, we need to consider the story of Mark.

> Mark was a young man of thirty-two from a family of Asian parents who had moved to the UK after marrying. His father was a successful entrepreneur whose business was a mystery to his whole family. Mark had been successful at school but felt that he had never managed to please his father. He was the only boy and felt that he had a secure place with his mother, which would not be questioned no matter what he did or did not do.

> Mark was a successful accountant with a number of clients although he was still young. He had been told that his firm might make him a partner in time. Despite all this acclaim, he was painfully unhappy and self-conscious. He felt that something terrible was about to happen and as he talked it became clear that something terrible already had happened. He had separated from his girlfriend when she would not give up her job to come and live in the town where he worked. He had spent many hours travelling to London where she worked in order to spend a few hours with her at weekends.

This was not his only problem, but it had become the reason he cited to himself for saying to her in an e-mail that he thought they should bring their relationship to an end.

Since this time, he had become more and more depressed and was not able to pull himself out of it. He reached the point where he could no longer go in to his office and face the meetings with clients. His boss was out of his depth and sent him to a psychiatrist who recommended psychotherapy and anti-depressants. Mark came to see a psychotherapist, feeling deeply shamed of the need to seek help because he was in a position that he could not sort out for himself. He made a beginning with an experienced female therapist, Martha M. At first he was very silent and seemed resentful of her position as the therapist. He came late by five or ten minutes to almost every session with good reasons at first. The good reasons began to fade and at last he came to a session just saying sadly, "I don't seem to dare get here on time". The therapist was surprised that such an admission of emotional presence had been made and just said, "So getting here really means something to you?" Mark said nothing, but in the next session, to which he had come more or less on time, he said that he had been thinking about what Martha had said in the previous session. She waited. There was a long pause. "It's no good. I can't say what the matter is. It's too difficult. I feel as though I'll explode I'm sorry. You're not helping me. I'm off." He stood up and exploded out of the room.

Martha was surprised and very unhappy. She waited for him in the next session but he did not appear, and she had to recognise that he was probably not going to return. She wrote him a brief letter in which, unlike Ellen's therapist, she just said that she was sorry not to have seen him and hoped to see him next week. She spoke to her supervisor and considered what could have been so unbearable for him. Between them they came to the conclusion that he was becoming more attached to Martha than he could bring himself to acknowledge. He found himself beginning to love her and to feel dependent on her view of him for his own peace of mind and self-image. That is a frightening level of connection to another person, and Mark's experience had been such that he had been important to his mother and had needed to be important to his therapist. His girlfriend had not been willing to give up her life for him so he did not expect his therapist to be willing to move from her place to show love or concern for him. Yet for him there could be no love unless it was like the profound admiration of his mother.

If Mark had been able to bear to show his therapist more of what he was feeling, he might have been able to reach a more manageable way of loving a woman in which he could let her have her own life, and yet believe that she could love and care for him.

This is the sort of ending that creates a high level of wear and tear on the therapist, who wishes to try to understand what happened. Most therapists would be trying to work out the extent to which they were to blame for the explosive ending. There is always something else that could have been said and some greater level of understanding that could have been shown. Fortunately we can never know what would have happened if the therapist had said something else, but many suffer considerably from agonising over it. Often there is some useful learning that can be discovered when intensive attention is given to the last phase of such a therapy. In this case, the therapist needs to consider what she knew of the patient's history. He had experienced a mother who was strongly supportive and always on his side. She could perhaps have said something about the enforced abstinence of the therapy situation in which he is not going to know what his therapist is thinking.

This approach to the question of what happened for Mark relies heavily on the theory of transference. The trouble is that, as Freud saw clearly, the playground of the transference is useful only in so far as the therapist can prevent the repetition from becoming so destructive that it cannot be interpreted. There are many ways in which this can happen but leaving is the most definitive. This is because "the transference thus creates an intermediate region between illness and real life through which the transition from one to the other is made". (Freud, 1915, p. 154) If that is true, the therapist may console herself with the knowledge that the patient will get better only through the transference. On the other hand, the path through it is bound to be long and beset with all sorts of difficulties, where the patient may lose hold of the thread that leads through the dark forest of painful feelings.

Freud knew how much this transference enactment may hurt the therapist, but "If he holds fast to this conviction he will often be spared the illusion of having failed when in fact he is conducting the treatment on the right lines". (Ibid, p. 155) Narcissistic needs in the therapist are not often discussed but are the subject of a paper by Stanley Coen. (Coen, 2007) Coen argues that narcissistic needs are "temptations" or "vulnerabilities". They can lead to boundary violations. Coen differentiates analysts into two types: those who may violate boundaries and those will never do so. (Ibid, p. 1171) In this case, the patient had experienced the kind of upbringing that Coen says presents a danger for analysts who, as children, were over indulged with no clear setting of limits. They feel entitled to keep repeating with patients their childhood Oedipal and pre-Oedipal scenes. Perhaps the patient recognised in himself the lack of the firm boundaries that might have been established in childhood. Because of this, he was able to imagine the same lack of boundaries in his therapist.

A second way of considering the possible reasons for Mark's departure would be to think in terms of envy. The moment when his therapist seemed to understand his feelings, perhaps better than he did himself, was the moment when he could not bear to stay. A Kleinian at this point would be thinking in terms of envy. "Envy is the angry feeling that another person possesses and enjoys something desirable – the envious impulse being to take it away or to spoil it." (Klein, 1975, p. 181) If a patient begins to feel that the therapist owns the equivalent of the feeding breast which is therefore not under his control, he may attack or simply disparage the interpretation that has brought him comfort. He then cannot bear to stay, and finally may destroy the source of help that is owned and controlled by the therapist. Mark's therapist would need to consider whether there could be any grounds for considering envy to be at the root of his difficulties. Of course she cannot do anything about it unless he returns and is willing to see the darker part of himself.

This view of the difficulty is close to what is often called "negative therapeutic reaction" (see also Chapter Four). Freud wrote of this phenomenon, in which a person cannot allow an improvement which might be a problem caused by envy of the generous feeding breast. (Freud, 1926a) It might also be caused by the agency of the superego, which responds to unconscious guilt by refusing to allow an improvement. In Mark's case, we might consider that he is seeing a female therapist who reminds him that he has already taken a great deal from his mother, but has never been able to please his father enough. If he allows himself to stay and take more from his mother in the transference, he may be afraid that he is removing himself even further from his father's approval. So maybe he is leaving to find a way to get closer to his father. Just maybe the therapist could have helped by saying something along those lines. If that had been said, it might have been the beginning of a lengthy piece of work. The problem of the negative therapeutic reaction will be considered in the next chapter because the therapist's mental state may lie at the heart of it as much as that of the patient.

The therapist's loss

Therapists have to face their fear of death and decline every time a patient leaves. This is not only the case with the difficult endings when only the patient chooses the time of ending, but is also a part of the more considered endings that are agreed, and even welcomed, by the therapist.

Dependency

Freud's own mortality was a blow to those who had developed an almost religious faith in his theory, and his ability to develop it further. During the second year of the First World War, in 1916, Freud wrote a description of a walk that he had taken before the war with two friends in the Dolomites in which they were all affected by the beauty of the landscape. His two friends were both sad to see it, being aware of its transience, and from this, Freud developed a reflection on mourning and our human sorrow for the people and experiences that we lose. He posed to himself the problem of why it should

53

be so painful to us to detach our libido from the objects that we have lost. He concluded:

> Mourning as we know comes to a spontaneous end. When it has renounced everything that has been lost, then it has consumed itself and our libido is once more free... to replace these objects with fresh ones equally or still more precious.... (Freud, 1917, p. 207)

In learning about loss, the story of Freud's cancer shows many of the characteristics that afflict us all as therapists when endings are in view. Peter Gay describes the onset of the cancer with clarity. (Gay, 1988) As a doctor, Freud knew only too well that the painful lesion on his palate was probably an epithelioma, a malignant growth, probably caused by smoking. Thus he knew that his own end could not be far away.

Glen Gabbard gives us an illustration of the therapist's desire. He does not tell us how it relates to his own past experience but the fantasy of pleasure and satisfaction relates to earlier experiences of what had given him pleasure.

> As she recounted her experience with this unhappy patient, I detected in myself a rather embarrassing and certainly naive fantasy that the analysis would end with a long awaited pregnancy, followed by the birth of a healthy baby. The analysis would then terminate with a grateful patient who would live happily ever after.
>
> Near the end of the analyst's presentation, I learned that the patient terminated as she began—childless. I was dismayed. I felt disappointed, even deprived. I wanted the ending that I wanted, even though I knew it was unlikely that talking to someone for a few years would change the function of that person's reproductive system. (Gabbard, 1995, p. 235-236)

Freud's own practice in the conduct of his analyses was to keep them short. In his view, an analysis that lasted six months was long. Research into Freud's own cases showed that the majority lasted less than 250 hours:

> Some cases lasted only a few months. Above all, Freud was pragmatic. Many ended at the beginning of his nearly three-month summer

holiday. He started some analyses knowing that the person would
be in the city for only a short time. May notes that only one or two
of Freud's patients were in truly open-ended analyses. (Ibid, p. 580)

Freud took on new patients in 1939 when he was already weak and
barely recovering from yet another operation to remove the recru-
descent cancer. They were inevitably going to have a very short analysis. Even when he was clearly very weak and in great pain, he still
kept a "few analytic hours whenever the pain did not torment him
too much". (Gay,1988, p. 648) Gay wrote that "an air of farewell hung
over those fall days and months" at the end of 1938. (Ibid., p.636) In
the end, Freud's physician, Max Schur, administered doses of mor-
phine which he needed for pain control but which were high enough
to bring an end to his suffering. "The old stoic had kept control of his
life to the end". (Ibid., p. 651)

In this way, Freud's own ending shows us that even terrible pain
can be faced with dignity, but also that he needed his doctor to understand that the time had come to help him and ease his passage
out of the life that was no longer bearable to him. He had very much
wanted to see all his works translated into English, especially "Mo-
ses and Monotheism" which was translated by Katherine Jones. Here
was both the wish to know that his work would not be lost and the
desire to make himself known in the future, as well as his profound
dependence on his daughter, Anna, and on the doctor who was treat-
ing him but was much more a friend than a professional..

In his critical biography of Freud, Peter Gay (Gay, 1988) does not
refer to the nature or fate of the analyses that Freud conducted in
these last years. How would it have been if one had been a patient of
an analyst who would be available only when his pain was not too
great? Freud's patients must have learned the value of their own au-
tonomy during this difficult period. Even if the analysis had been
concluded, there would inevitably still have been work that would
not have been done. The terminated patient is not "fully analysed"–
he or she is simply embarking on a life of self-analytic reflection that
offers depth and richness to one's existence. Suffering, intrapsychic
conflict, and problems in work and love will continue. A tragic vision is
central to the psychoanalytic journey. (Gabbard, 1995, p. 585–586).

If psychoanalytic theory has any validity, the therapist must be subject to its power just as much as the patient. If we follow this train of thought to its conclusion, we have to accept that the experience of endings of all sorts will be present for the therapist, and will affect how she approaches and deals with the endings that her patients need to investigate and experience. If human beings are prone to introject, or later to identify, with people whom they have lost, then previous patients will affect the way in which the therapist can allow an ending. Perhaps reclaiming the part of the ego that has become identified with previous loss will be, Freud finally argued, the only way we are able to accept the loss of a significant object (Freud,1917).

In his letters to Oskar Pfister in the 1920s, Freud continued to work against the prevalence of religion and the religious defences against the fear of death. His own cancer was affecting his general health and made him aware of his own impending death, and perhaps his wish that he could accept religious consolation. If he were to manage without that, he would have to confirm his own theory to his own satisfaction.

In 1923, Marcus Hajek performed an operation to remove the growth from Freud's jaw. He was a rhinologist and Gay implies that Freud already knew that his growth was malignant. His friend and former student, Felix Deutsch, accompanied him and both tried to treat the removal as a trivial occasion. In fact it turned into a very bad experience after which Freud bled uncontrollably and nearly died. After this operation in 1923, Freud's friends, who in many cases were qualified doctors, did not refer to his lesion as cancer. Deutsch must have known what was there, but "a certain awe before the great man and a wishful unwillingness to accept his mortality" (Gay, 1988, p. 421) may have prevented him from recognising what he could see.

Freud at this time also suffered from depression, and was even possibly suicidal. Gay tells us that Deutsch refrained from openly discussing the nature of the illness because he thought that Freud's heart might not stand it, but also that he had asked to be helped to "'disappear from the world with decency' if he should be condemned to prolonged suffering". (Gay, 1988, p.421) There were other reasons for depression. His beloved grandson, Heinele, died of tuberculosis. The little boy was only four, and he died in June after Freud's shocking operation. This took away any pleasure which he might have found in life before that. He said that he was then experiencing depression. "I never had a depression before but this must be one". (Freud, 1988, p. 422) Suicidal ideas returned in the dark days of Nazi oppression in Vienna in 1938. Anna Freud asked him on one occasion if it would not be better that they should all kill themselves, as many others did. Freud's reply was "Why? Because they would like us to?" (Freud, 1988, p. 622) He was capable of resilience, and although his defiance was based more on hope than a realistic appraisal of the situation in Austria, we can see that he had overcome the depression enough to continue to practise psychoanalysis.

In the summer of 1923, Freud took his daughter to Rome but he was suffering more and more because of his jaw, and it was clear that he needed another operation. Over the coming years, he suffered about thirty minor operations to remove recurrent lesions and precancerous growths. He also had a prosthesis fitted which caused him considerable pain from the fitting, refitting and cleaning. His speech was difficult and distorted and his hearing also suffered. He was working with patients and moved the position of the couch so that he would hear them better. He thought that his speech was still intelligible to his friends, family, and to patients.

This account of the difficulties that Freud suffered shows us the problems in facing the end of life, both our own, and that of those we love or admire. He understood this difficulty well in principle. He explained our respect for the dead in part as our reluctance to acknowledge that death is a fact. He points out that, in the unconscious, there is no possible representation of our death. We are always present in some way as an observer. For this reason, we do not behave as though a dead person had really gone. We continue to maintain the need to speak well—de mortuis nil nisi bonum ("of the dead, nothing but good", attributed to Chilon of Sparta). He thought that the war would change this however. We would no longer be able to deny the reality of death when people died in their hundreds. (Freud, 1915) In this perhaps he was wrong. Defences are more necessary than ever in such terrible times.

In 1926, the pain from the prosthesis was very bad and Freud worried that he would no longer be able to work. He said that he feared not being able to earn, and there is no doubt that this was a strong consideration. However, he did also need to be able to feel that his life work was continuing. He had written to Otto Rank on accepting the dedication of a book *non omnis moriar* ("I shall not altogether die" —a quotation from Horace's *Ode* 3.30). One of the difficulties of ending from the therapist's position is certainly the fear of dying. The death that is feared is not only the physical death of the body, but the death of the professional self. Freud bolstered his wish to go on working by pointing out that he still needed to support his family. On the other hand, he kept alive his own view of himself as a practising psychoanalyst. This, to a greater or lesser extent, is present for people facing retirement. The question at a social event, "what do you do?", is easily answered by the working professional, but can become a matter of shame and hesitation for those who are considering retirement. I wished to find out whether this is in fact the case through interviews (see Chapter Six) with those who have retired and are not merely anticipating how they might feel in the future. The question is usually put by someone who is trying to find a subject for conversation, and when the answer is a role in society of some sort (e.g., "I'm a doctor" or "I'm a teacher") it can lead on to a conversation perhaps about the current issues for the professions. On the other hand, saying "I'm a retired teacher" could still lead to reminiscence, but the working teacher fears that it might not be as interesting or as likely to lead to respect.

How do therapists protect themselves from the reality of death and loss? Before he was faced with the imminence of his own death, Freud spent a considerable time demolishing the comfort of religion, and therefore also the comfort that it brings to the person facing an ending, particularly an ending caused by death. He thought in developmental terms, assigning the religious attitude to the obsessional stage in which there is a predominance of magical thinking and wish fulfilment. Kung (Kung, 1979) argues that even if we accept that this view of religious thinking is valid, it tells us nothing about the truth or validity of the view. What, he asks, is wrong with wishing and making up a story that fulfils those wishes?

Morgan Rempel argues for an open attitude to religious truth:

> While I cannot agree with all aspects of Kung's assessment of Freud's philosophy of religion, I wholeheartedly agree with his

reasoned observation that Freud's study of the wish-fulfilling character of religious belief, even if wholly accurate, by no means demonstrates that these same religious beliefs are groundless, that God does not exist, and that eternal life and happiness are not realities. As Kung (1979) stated:

Perhaps this being of our longings and dreams does actually exist. Freud's explanation of the psychological genesis of belief in God did not refute this faith itself" (pp. 79–80). Very true. (Rempel, 1997, p. 231)

Perhaps the therapist has to undergo something similar in her own body and/or mind. Losses and endings are not alien to any of us and our own experience, as we know, must be involved in whatever we are experiencing with clients. The therapist has to impose endings on her patients even when she does not wish to do so. Usually, quite willingly, she ends sessions and ends a period of work in order to take a necessary or desired holiday. The feelings in her own self, and the way she shows them to her patients, will be a preparation for both of them for the final ending which is usually imposed by the patient, but sometimes needs to come from the therapist. The rest of this chapter will consider some examples of endings where the therapist was not fully aware of her own process, and will look in detail at the outcome for the patient.

Some analysts may counterphobically or even prematurely suggest that the analysis should end to evade superego pressure that they are exploiting the patient for their own purposes. (Gabbard, 1995, p. 588)

Apart from situations in which illness or external circumstances, such as a partner's job, make moving necessary, the therapist may sometimes consider bringing therapy to an end for intrinsic reasons. If a patient has stayed with a therapist out of fear of ending for reasons that have remained unconscious, the result may be a prolonged but unproductive therapy. The therapist may need to consider ending but most often the ending will be brought about by her external circumstances by moving away or changing work arrangements.

Independence

For some people, a growing awareness of the importance of the therapist to them is a danger signal that they cannot ignore. The human infant is delighted to be admired and to show off to adults his ability to stand or to say his first words. He enjoys this but at the same time, he tries desperately to achieve independence, to be able to stand without an adult to support him and to bring about enough independence to feel autonomous within the bounds of the safety of his parents or caregivers' attention. The patient in therapy is both an infant re-experiencing the joy of demonstrating his strength and prowess, and also an adult. He knows that he must eventually seek independence and be left to manage alone. He also can feel that this will not be easy. He has enjoyed being watched and, he may feel, approved by his therapist. All of this can produce a straightforward fear about continuing with a process that leads further and further into a devotion which seems to carry the danger of dependence. Therapists can recognise this situation in a variety of ways and may need to speak about it:

> Joseph had been seeing a female therapist for three years. His initial reason for consulting her was a lack of confidence in his teaching, which made him terrified of certain classes. The therapist, Mrs B, had been a teacher herself, and though she did not say this, he understood that she was able to feel for his difficulties. She also had, occasionally, something very practical to say about the management of a particular situation. She began to feel anxious that the sessions were turning into a sort of tutorial and that she was no longer being analytic. One day Joseph said, "I find what you say very useful and I don't know why I can't come up with these ideas myself". Mrs B realised that the time had come when she must say something. "Perhaps I have been too useful and my thoughts and ideas have intruded and prevented you from thinking these situations through as well as you could. I might be putting you in the position of the young child who thinks that only his father knows how to play football". Joseph had said that he had never played football because his father was so good at it that he could never compete. He had little to say at that point but he began, in subsequent sessions, to put forward his own ideas, and when she remained silent, he began to critique them himself.

This account shows that a potentially difficult ending can be avoided and the therapist opens the possibility of an ending that does not damage the self and is driven by self-respect.

Therapists bereaved

Dealing with loss has always been a major part of the theoretical and technical requirement of a clinician who intends to embark on any kind of analytic work. A therapist who has never experienced loss is unlikely to be as helpful as one who has. This is where the bereavement of the whole profession in the loss of the early theorists provides a backdrop of experience from which all can draw. The individual therapist has to throw off the dead hand of the lost person and begin again to live. Freud's own pre-analytic comment is still applicable: "much will be gained if we succeed in transforming ... hysterical misery into common unhappiness". (Breuer and Freud, 1895, p. 305)The story of Ellen described in Chapter Two shows how a personal tragedy, usually a loss of some sort, can lead to a reactive depression. This we can see and recognise in the patient, but when there is a formal complaint, we begin to focus more closely on the effect of depression on the therapist. Clearly there is no doubt that the therapist must put the patient's wellbeing first at all times. This is all very well in principle, but in practice few of us would be able to say that it is always the case. Personal mental states make a difference, and the therapist has an unconscious just as the patient does. The difference is that she is obliged to try to understand its workings in the relationship.

The therapist's state of mind will affect the way in which she manages the needs of her patient. The profession as a whole is well aware of this, and puts ethical requirements on us all to consult when we know that we are finding a particular patient difficult. This is not a panacea, and the therapist who is being tested by a patient may well be in the most difficult position to accept and manage the patient's distress. In the case of Ellen's therapist, Jane, we might all empathise with the distress of the therapist for leaving her mother in such a state of severe illness. Jane came back to the UK in order to see her patients when she was still very concerned about her mother's health.

She might have unconsciously expected gratitude from patients who in reality did not know of her sacrifice. This is an element that can enter into a therapeutic relationship if it is left to be unconscious in the therapist.

An unconscious sense that the patient should be grateful will of course play into the mother or father transference for many people.

Maria says her mother is the most selfish woman that ever lived. She remembered that as a child of six or seven she had badly wanted a kitten, but her parents said it would be too much trouble. She was a lonely child with no brothers or sisters but was told the story of a miscarried baby before she was born. One day, she remembers her father came from work with a kitten. She was almost unable to believe that such a wonderful thing had happened. She kept the kitten for two or three weeks, but her mother developed a severe allergy to its fur and her father said that they would have to give it away. She remembers the utter devastation and distress of giving up the kitten.

"You blamed your mother for her allergy?" asked the therapist.

"I hated her for it. The worst thing was that she demanded that I should be grateful for everything she did for me. She wouldn't just give me a piece of cake, it was always: 'Wasn't that a lovely cake I made for you?'"

"Perhaps", said the therapist, "your mother felt guilty and wanted to make it up to you."

Maria was silent at this and it formed an unresolved question and theme in the work for some time. When it came to the time when Maria said that she was moving to another job and would have to end her therapy, the therapist, Ms J, felt that she had done some good work. She looked forward to the last session in which she thought that Maria might say something about the value of the sessions to her. In fact, the last session came and Maria was silent and appeared to be angry. Her therapist did not recognise that in her attitude and some of her comments, she had taken the place of the mother who was felt to be depriving her of something of great value, even though of course Maria was the one causing the ending. On top of that, she said, "We have done some useful work and of course missed some things. Nevertheless, you might feel that the good things outnumber the ones we have missed." Maria was silent and perhaps she heard this as a request for gratitude. The trouble was that Ms J was actually feeling that gratitude would be appropriate and was hoping, or even expecting, that Maria would express it in some way.

Unless the therapist can stop and recognise what she is doing, the patient will be unlikely to find a way of expressing her true feeling. Since it was very near the moment of parting, the time for working with this would have been very limited, and Maria may have kept silent to avoid damaging the therapist beyond repair.

Maria might have reached a positive feeling for the therapist but probably had to go through a recognition of the negative. Sometimes the positive feelings alone are enough to lead to a difficult ending. In order to consider the position of the patient who leaves because of a positive attachment to the therapist, we need to return to consider the story of Mark from Chapter Two.

Mark's therapist was faced with the fact that he was a man whom she found attractive. She was willing to acknowledge this to her supervisor and would never act on it. The danger for the patient arose, not from any conscious response to him, but from her unconscious responses. We know that patients envy the therapist for her ability to sit calmly and for all sorts of imagined success: her work and her family and her ability to be helpful. This envy is gratifying because it gives the patient a feeling that he can find some power to act. It is gratifying to the therapist because it conveys a picture of something desirable. Although the patient's fantasies about the happiness of the personal life may be wide of the mark, the belief that the therapist is an ideal practitioner is gratifying, even if a part of the therapist manages to remember that this is a form of transference, and is based on a need of the patient rather than reality. How does a person react to this? —Often with discomfort and an awareness that the bubble of admiration that grows above the envy must burst at some point. Sometimes the patient is disillusioned too quickly and leaves. If this idealisation and consequent envy continue, they will lead to a sense of grandiosity in the therapist, unless she feels the appropriate reaction of discomfort.

The therapist's own envy of the patient is more difficult to address but is very important in leading to unhelpful endings. Why should a therapist envy a patient? There might be many reasons for such feelings, but there are some that will be common. Many therapists give up their own personal therapy when their training is over. They may well envy the patient who is able to have the luxury of time and attention. The more work the patient is able to achieve, the more the therapist might feel pleased on the surface and envious under that. An outsider would ask why the therapist would not go back into therapy in those circumstances. There might be many reasons for this, not least that the therapist might not recognise her envy and longing to get such attention for herself. Even if she does, she will often dismiss her need because she also knows about the emotional demands of being a patient. She may feel that she cannot cope with this and with her patients' needs at the same time. Many therapists of course do go back into therapy and work on their own reactions to seeing patients. The deleterious effect of continuing to manage without therapy might show in the patient as a feeling that something is wrong, but he is not sure what it is. The feeling for him will be caused by the contradiction of the mother who says one thing and means another. The term given to this in the past was *schizophrenogenic* This mother is pulling the child towards her saying "I love you and you are just the child I want" and then she pushes him away: "Go away. I'm tired or busy and I don't find you desirable at all".

A patient who is faced with a therapist experiencing negative feelings beneath the surface will have no way of understanding what is happening, any more than the small child can know what opposing forces are working in his mother. Leaving the therapist and therefore the confusion of this state may seem to be the only option and may be, obscurely, a relief for the therapist as well.

Therapists try not to impose their own emotional difficulties onto their patients, and may seek to do so by exaggerated offerings to them. Mark's therapist used the altruistic defence in trying to work out some of her negative feelings about her own mother by being extra helpful and generous to her patients. An illustration of this possibility arises in some therapists who are seeing patients on Mondays. In the UK, there are several public holidays that occur on Mondays. I have heard a therapist comment, "I shall be working on the second public holiday because my Monday people have missed enough." Often there is a good clinical reason for the patient to have a session and not to miss so much more than their siblings, who come for therapy on other days. This is an admirable impulse and may be nothing more than useful to the patients concerned. On the other hand, it may be given with an undertone of requirement for gratitude or even an undertone of resentment. The whole experience of the demanding, emotionally impoverished mother may be unintentionally conveyed to the patient. The therapist, as always, will have to wake up to what she is doing and put some of it into words.

Negative therapeutic reaction

In the patient, there may be some resilience which can lead either to leaving in disappointment, or to a refusal to accept that there is nothing more. This patient will refuse to allow that he is better and will not accept the good things that the therapist is able to give him, in spite of her own difficulties. The negative therapeutic reaction is a signal to the therapist that there are unresolved anxieties which may arise from the therapist's own behaviour, or from narcissistic problems. The patient is trying to internalise a good object, but is confronted with the risks of seeking to manage it alone. This might imply a risk to the safety of the good object. Continuing the analytic work may seem like the safest place for it. In other words, staying with the physical presence of the therapist may seem like the only way to avoid the risk of destroying her. The mother may already have been damaged in thought and word, and there is fear of doing the same to the therapist. This raises the question of whether the patient perceives some anxiety in the therapist. Not surprisingly, therapists do sometimes fear being bereft by the loss of the patient. On the other hand, the patient is likely to fantasise that his absence will matter to the therapist, and he will be captured by the ambivalence of wanting this to be so and fearing it.

In this way, the therapist's fear of loss becomes the patient's resistance to it. This can be problematic as the therapist is only too happy to collude with delaying the ending, and is doing so because neither is yet ready for ending. The trouble is that difficult work, usually involving the acknowledgement of negative feelings, will need to be done. Therapists need to be able to face this and be confident that it does not leave the patient with only negative feelings but may enable more secure positive feelings in the end. Manic defences are usually popular because they begin by being enjoyable. Only when the mania becomes apparent is the individual ready to consider living without this defence. A successful ending requires both to be willing to accept that loss is part of the human condition, and that sadness may be more appropriate than frantic attempts to hide it through more work.

CHAPTER FIVE

The trouble with ending

Defences against loss

The previous chapter considered the ways in which the patient may echo and suffer from the therapist's fear of loss. This chapter will consider some of the ways in which the therapist and the patient seek to manage the distress of loss. Patients and therapists face losses of all sorts in their lives. No wonder that one of the most useful provisions of therapy is the opportunity to endure a loss with sadness and some anger, but without the full blown persecution of the paranoid schizoid position.

Melanie Klein pointed out the pain of the infant or small child on losing the good breast. (Klein, 1940) Watching a small infant fall asleep at the breast helps us to understand this pain which begins at the very outset. Most mothers are cautious about removing themselves gently from the sleeping infant to put her down to sleep. A sudden deprivation will lead to an outcry rather than a peaceful transition into sleep. The emotional experience of loss at this moment seems to involve a mixture of fear and rage. The disturbed infant seems to feel "I have lost something which I may never have again." Klein also describes this emotion as giving rise to guilt. The infant, in her all-embracing narcissistic view of the world, is likely to have the idea that she has caused the deprivation that is so painful. If this is the case, the baby will have guilt mixed with her anger when she begins to understand that the mother who feeds her and loves her is a separate person, and is capable of being damaged by her hunger.

This Kleinian emphasis on the infant's phantasy of exhausting the breast and leaving the mother empty and useless is relevant to the guilt that often seems to accompany the wish to end.

> Ira was a young male patient who was moving to a new job in another city. He had to leave his therapist, but the main loss that he seemed in agony to contemplate was leaving his work mates to continue without him. Certainly he worked in an area of social work that was already understaffed, and he had reason to think that his loss would be a blow to the department. Yet his guilt seemed extreme.
>
> It took a while for his therapist to understand that leaving her (which was hardly mentioned) was the subject that needed to be addressed.
>
> The therapist understood that his phantasy was that he was leaving her empty and exhausted and unable to continue without him. This had to be faced and gradually addressed so that even if she were to retire or grow ill, it would not be because he had left her. Finally, there would be the wish to be so important to her that she would not be able to survive without him emotionally. This is often difficult for therapists because the patient has become important to them in all sorts of ways beyond making a living.
>
> Although denial is often a favourite first line of defence, there comes a point, as it did for Ira, when the therapist wakes up to the painful subject that is being denied and sees that she must address it. Patients usually give some clue that there is an understanding, even if it is quite well hidden. Ira was happy to talk about other partings that he had endured and how difficult he had found it when left by someone important. He had parted from a girlfriend some time before, and even though he had met someone new, he still worried about what he had done to his previous girlfriend. In fact, she had

made the move to separate and it was not originated by him, and yet he felt responsible for her survival, both financially and because "she just is helpless when I am not there."

Since this kind of bereavement is one that therapists have to face as an ordinary part of their working lives, it is clearly important to stop and think of the elements that are mixed up in any ending. The whole profession faces bereavements at times. The previous chapter explored some of the ways in which the fathers and mothers of the profession faced ending. Freud himself did not end his working life until he was physically incapable of continuing. Joan Riviere was forced to stop attending meetings of the British Psychoanalytic Society due to ill health, not by any choice that she might have made because she wished to retire. Others such as Charles Rycroft died *in medias res* while still in possession of their working lives. (Pearson, 2004)

Why are therapists particularly prone to hold on to the possibility of working? Why are they not as eager as anyone else to sleep late, go on holiday when they feel like it, sprawl in the sun reading a novel? Some in fact do plan to do all these things and look forward to them but are still not eager to make it happen tomorrow. The conclusion seems to be that the continuing work is providing a defence against a deeper fear. That fear does not seem to be easy to acknowledge. All kinds of losses are connected to the loss of stopping working, even just with one person. Mélanie Klein is perhaps one of the earliest theorists who worked with loss. She understood its importance to the young child and was able to put it in context. She saw that there are losses involved in weaning and in the growing independence of the child who has to recognise the existence of the father. Activity of all sorts, and for many adults work itself, can be a manic defence when losses are threatening the immature ego. Mélanie Klein described the depressive position attained by most children in their first year. This description might be relevant to the therapist who is contemplating the ending for a long term patient, and who has come to sessions long enough to become a known and important element in the therapist's life:

When the depressive position arises the ego is forced (in addition

to earlier defences) to develop methods of defence which are essentially directed against the pining for the loved object...

Omnipotence, denial and idealization, closely bound up with ambivalence enable the early ego to assert itself to a certain degree
against its internal persecutors and against a slavish and perilous
dependence upon its loved objects and thus to make further ad-
vances in development. (Klein, 1940, p. 349)

This is a way of describing the impact on the safety and security of
the therapist caused by the potential loss of a patient. Like the patient, she must then confront the fear and rework the resolution
which she has already experienced in infancy.

Each of the three defences named by Klein can be seen in a therapist's response to the possibility of ending.

Omnipotence

If a patient achieves enough self-confidence to discuss ending and
tries to seek to negotiate it with the therapist, reactions vary. Some
therapists will not be sure of their own view. Is this person ready to
end or not? For many this is appropriate doubt and they will perhaps consult their supervisors. Others will claim to know all the answers. Pronouncements about leaving as a defence or leaving to avoid
the breakthrough that is just on the horizon may be close to the mark,
but if pronouncements are delivered with a conviction of being right,
they may be harmful. The therapist will think that she knows whether
the wish to end is defensive and will not always have sufficient evidence to interpret defences . The patient has the option of staying
and feeling ashamed of his level of compliance, or feeling resentful.
In either of those cases, he is not likely to continue to improve. In
fact, he is most likely to develop an inner refusal to change or improve in order to prevent the therapist from reaping any reward for
behaviour which will probably echo the apparent power of the parent.

If the patient refuses to accept the therapist's demand that he
should stay in therapy longer, he is faced with the option of walking
out without the blessing of his therapist. This may repeat other bad

or unsatisfactory endings.

> Robert was a young gay man who came to see a female therapist, Dr Allen. He had grown up an only child whose mother idolised him. His father was a salesman who was often away. He had told his mother that he realised he was gay as an adolescent. She accepted that and in fact seemed pleased about it. During the therapy, it emerged that she might have been pleased because no other woman was to take her place. Robert was shocked about this understanding, but he could see that her words and actions bore it out. He was unable to form a lasting relationship with a man and had described many one night stands when he enjoyed the risks of gay sex without relationship.

> He told his therapist that he might as well leave because clearly she could not help him find a satisfying relationship. Dr Allen was very concerned and told him that she thought he was avoiding staying and working through his anger with his mother. He then became very angry with Dr Allen and walked out.

The sad thing about this story is that Dr Allen was probably right, but she merely exacerbated the anger and did not provide enough possibility of enabling Robert to feel that his anger could be managed in a non-lethal way.

Denial

Dr Allen's response to Robert also demonstrates something of the power of denial as a defence against loss. She might have been able to understand the possible effect of her response to him, but she did not wish to acknowledge the validity or the strength of his feeling. He was confronting her with a despair which would have been very difficult to accept. She was being asked to enter into his feeling that he could not be helped with the one change that he thought was important to make him feel better. She would have to allow herself to be useless in that context, and would have to find her own self-respect in some other aspect of the work, either with Robert or with someone else. No therapist likes it when all she can do is allow the patient to tell her that it is all hopeless. Winnicott described an occasion when he acknowledged to a patient that he could see no hope. Yet he continued with the analysis. (Winnicott, 1960, p. 152) Paradoxically, it was only then that the patient was able to find hope and move forward, because his analyst was not afraid to face this most frightening experience.

The analyst who believes that there will always be value in continuing with therapeutic work, regardless of how helpful the patient thinks it is, might deny the patient the ability to face loss and the pain that goes with it. This inability to face being of no further use is a denial of something that the therapist suspects to be true. Of course there is always the problem that we can never know for certain what will be helpful and what will not. Sometimes the patient is most helped by an acknowledgement of uncertainty in which the therapist shows that she can bear the not knowing. In order for it to be helpful rather than just confusing, the therapist needs to be able to face the possibility of a narcissistic wound and sense of personal failure that is involved if none of the work seems to be of any use. Here, an understanding of the workings of grandiosity and omnipotence are helpful. The therapist does not know at any point exactly what the effect of her work can be. To assume that she knows either that it was or was not useful involves a kind of grandiosity.

Patients and therapists may both retreat into a premature denial of what the therapy could mean. One of the characteristics of the manic state is a contempt which is often mobilised to render the therapist's words useless and harmless. One of the difficulties that Dr Allen experienced with Robert was that he told her that she was no help in a tone of voice which she found hurtful. She was not a naturally assertive person and she found herself withdrawing and wanting to give up. One effect of this response was to activate the contempt in her. She was able to deal with Robert's rejection of her words by thinking that he was highly defended. She even believed in her innermost self that he was too stupid to understand what she was saying to him. She probably would not have admitted that even to herself, but it was not surprising that this painful and possibly damaging response was evoked in her since he was seeking to avoid it in himself.

Other difficult endings are brought about by denial of the importance of a good outcome. Sometimes a patient and therapist can join in a sort of cheerful collusion that there is an external reason for an ending. This might seem perfectly acceptable on the surface, but it will leave both people with an uncomfortable feeling that something was wrong. These will be endings that can echo early experiences of the absent or depressed mother who is unable to give her full attention to her child. The child grows up feeling more or less all right and is generally used to things not being as good as they might be. If this can be spoken by the therapist who understands this feeling, and is willing to admit to it with the patient, it can lead to a rescue. Whatever happens between the two in the time that remains is at least taking place between two people who are fully alive, and fully present to whatever there is between them.

Idealisation

Denial links closely to the defence of idealisation. The infant is terrified by the persecutions of hunger and abandonment when his mother is not immediately available to satisfy his needs, and he protects himself from these terrors by creating an idealised breast which makes all well. Klein described this as a defence developed by the ego in the very young infant. (Klein, 1975, p. 64) For the therapist, this idealised breast may be a gloriously successful analytic ability which will cure all ills. Although most therapists learn what is possible and what is not, and gradually become more realistic in their hopes and aspirations, nevertheless a tendency may resurface to idealise the power of the analytic method to enable patients to achieve something of their hopes before they leave. This may entail refusing to accept that it is time to accept that there is only a minimal level of achievement, which could still allow the patient to finish.

Harold Searles, in his seminal paper on Oedipal love in the analyst, quotes E. Weigert in order to critique her view of countertransference. She makes the point that the ending phase will bring out the countertransference:

> The termination of analysis is an experience of loss which mobilises all the resistances in the transference and in the counter transference too for a final struggle. (Searles, 1965, p. 286)

Searles' response to this is that the therapist must recognise not only a transference to the patient as a loved infant, but also a response to an adult at a genital level. (Ibid, p. 287) A defence against acting out the Oedipal love of the therapist might be an omnipotent determination to control the direction and timing of the therapy. This might lead to a wish to keep the loved object with her. There is likely to be a welter of confused feelings about letting the patient go.

Searles also points to the narcissistic element in the therapist who has found that her patient has improved. Maybe the patient has led her to some new thinking which she might even hope to publish. Even without publication, the sense of having achieved something useful for the patient can itself give rise to what Searles connects to the Pygmalion in the therapist who has created something new. (Ibid, p. 300) In Greek myth, Pygmalion is a sculptor who creates a statue of such beauty that he falls in love with her. He calls her Galatea and begs Venus to bring her to life. She does. There is sometimes something of the Pygmalion in the therapist who may lose her humility and begin to see herself as the creator of the charming human being who is emerging from the heat of the therapeutic process. Letting the patient go, or even encouraging the patient to feel that he can make an ending, is going to run counter to these elements in the therapist, who might have to learn that she will not be diminished but may in fact be enhanced by the loss of her patient.

Small wonder that for a therapist approaching old age and losses in her own life, continuing to work and retain the identity of a psychotherapist may be a form of manic defence which is difficult to give up. Klein points out that the manic defence is a reaction to the acceptance of our own potential to damage the loved object. At some level, the therapist who does not easily accept the need for ending is defending herself against the fear of causing harm. She will have achieved the depressive position in Kleinian terms, but will be assailed by the despair of knowing that not all harm comes from the outside—which is the fundamental belief of the paranoid position. This acceptance of the potential harm done by the envy and hatred of which we are all capable is a lifelong task and is not achieved once and for all, but must continue to be reworked throughout a professional life. (Klein, 1946)

Therapists approaching their sixties, seventies, and eighties are increasingly likely to have experienced losses as they grow older. Of a group of ten elderly therapists meeting together in 2013 in London to consider retirement, one had lost a partner in the last year and two had partners with life-threatening illnesses. Others had lost close friends, colleagues, or parents during the past year. All of this was accepted with professional equanimity but a great deal of personal pain. The group was aware that there would be an impact on the patients from this degree of loss. Some were able to think that the main impact would be positive. Patients suffering loss or impending loss would feel that their therapist had a profound understanding of what loss means.

Melanie is a young lawyer married to a newly qualified General Practitioner named Robert. He sounded affectionate but unavailable as he worked very long hours and even when he was at home he was worrying about the decisions that he had made. She was the much-loved only child of two academic parents. At school, she was successful and gave them the kind of academically successful child they seemed to want. The therapist, Mrs A, worked with Melanie on the fundamental insecurity that seemed to be the result of her belief that her father had wanted a boy. He never said so and Melanie remembered a kind and loving father. She had just a few hints, such as the kind of presents he gave her which she remembers as being always construction toys that she did not like or bother with. She knew that he wanted her to play with them and spend time making the sort of things that he said he had made in his childhood. She believed that he would have spent time with her if she had shown any interest, but she could not bring herself to do this. "It was the only thing he really wanted from me and I couldn't, wouldn't do it." The therapist said, "Maybe you felt that trying to do it would have made you into a sort of substitute boy, not a real boy but just an attempt at one." Melanie had paused over this and brought it back to later sessions, struggling over the question of whether she was even a real girl or just a pretend version, neither one thing nor the other.

In the second year of the therapy, Melanie came in to her session and burst into tears. "It's Robert. He has not been well recently but I thought he was just tired. He has pancreatic cancer. Apparently he had some tests and wouldn't tell me until he was sure. Now he is sure. He says they will try to operate but it is already metastatic and he thinks they probably should not even try. I suppose they will do what they possibly can for him. I think it is very rare for someone as young as he is to have this form of cancer. Or any form I think." She was making a great effort not to cry but she could not manage to say any more at this point. Mrs A was also near to tears. A close friend of hers had died of this sort of cancer just a few weeks earlier and she had just been to a memorial service. Partly because of her own closeness to breaking down, and partly because she believed it was needed, she stayed quiet for the rest of the session. She just showed by her attentiveness and the occasional slight encouragement, which was not much more than the repetition of what had last been said, that she was willing and able to hear this most painful communication.

There is very little that is more disturbing in human life than the anticipation of the death of those we love. Mrs A found listening to the approaching death of Melanie's husband one of the most difficult experiences of her professional life. Because she knew the nature of this sort of cancer from her own experience, she had no temptation to be unrealistically hopeful. Her difficulty was more along the lines of allowing Melanie to have her own unrealistic hopes. At one point, Melanie said that she thought that Robert seemed to be responding a little better to the chemotherapy. Maybe he was being helped by it. Mrs A knew that since the cancer was already metastatic, there was almost no chance that the chemotherapy would help, and indeed Robert had apparently told Melanie that himself.

Melanie came to the next session full of a sort of manic optimism. "I don't even know if he needs the rest of the chemo. He seems much better. I have decided that we must take this opportunity to spend time together. I will go away with him and we will have some time together. That means I will not be coming here anymore."

Mrs A was shocked. She felt that this was a manic defence, a form of avoidance of the inevitability of death. She was also very aware that taking away hope would be a form of cruelty, supposing that she had the power to do it. She decided to concentrate on the possibility of leaving the therapy precipitately. "I know that this is the place where you have talked about your most painful fears. It doesn't surprise me at all that you might believe that leaving here is like leaving those behind, at least for the time being. Perhaps you believed that your father would love only one part of you that could be strong and masculine and that I, on the other hand, will not want to see you if you are not always heart broken and wounded." Melanie immediately burst into tears and sobbed as if all her grief for her father and Robert were rolled into one.

The therapist's difficulties with Melanie's grief illustrates both how hard it can be to hear the story that is being told, and to keep hold of the other elements that may entangle themselves and make it more difficult for the patient to endure. Mrs A's own experience of loss made it harder to remain calm enough to hear the patient, but it also enabled the therapist to understand the patient's pain. This does not mean that she openly revealed her own distress. Some therapists sometimes do. In a large survey of US psychological therapists, Blume-Marcovici et al. (Blume-Marcovici, A., Stolberg, R., & Khademi, M., 2013) found that 72 per cent of the sample had cried during therapy on hearing some very sad story from the patient, where the meaning of "cried" ranged from tears welling up to sobbing. Surveys carried out in the UK have been smaller and less formal, but show a similar figure. After Blume-Marcovici's study had been reported in a BBC Radio 4 programme *All in the Mind*, broadcast on 15 May 2013, a number of patients contacted the programme to say that they had left therapy or changed therapists after their therapist had cried during a session, or said that she was feeling very distressed at the subject that the patient was bringing up. These people felt that they had to look after the therapist and be careful about what they said. These were not satisfactory endings. Commenting on these findings, some professionals were reported as saying that the therapists who cried seemed not to be doing their job of helping the patient to endure and manage intense feelings.

Winnicott writes of the same kind of difficulties, and yet he did not find it necessary to end an analysis. He emphasised the pleasure of the work as well as the commitment to finish what you have begun:

> Having begun an analysis I expect to continue with it, to survive it,
> and to end it. I enjoy myself doing analysis and I always look for-
> ward to the end of each analysis. (Winnicott, 1962, p. 166)

A difficult patient makes the ordinary therapist sometimes wish for
the ending. Can the therapist bring about the ending with a difficult
patient, or should she always wait for the patient to end? There are
precedents for the therapist ending even though most would regard
that as a last resort. The psychoanalyst, Masud Khan, describes a very
difficult patient who told him that she had met one of her previous
analysts and seduced him sexually. She felt terrible and she disturbed
Khan, who told her that she could not be helped in the analytic situation.

> Her language did not assimilate her experience, intrapsychic or
> interpersonal, any more than her body personalized her instincts
> or her affects. I realized that I had made a grave mistake in letting
> her take hold of the clinical space and process on her terms and run
> amok with it. I should have dosed the clinical process from the
> very beginning through infrequent consultations in the measure
> that she could tolerate them. I communicated this to her and in-
> formed her that I did not think I would now be able to correct my
> error and advised her to go to another analyst. After some vocifer-
> ous protestations, she did go to another colleague. (Khan, 1973, p.
> 236)

Khan felt that he could not convey just how bad this woman made
him feel. He thought that she would not recognise him as a person
and could not recognise her own self either. As a result she was driv-
ing herself to destruction.

When the twenty-four year old girl arrived in the sessions she refused to lie down, saying that she had never lain down. She had been
very difficult and had terrorised her previous female therapist by
breaking her furniture and even attacking her physically by pulling
her hair. Khan describes establishing a way of communicating with
this young woman so that she was able to see that symbolic discourse
could enable a kind of relating between two people.

When she came for the first session with Khan, she refused to talk. He
did not argue with this position and said that he could understand that

she was not able to use words to make contact. She would occasionally shout at him: "Say something. You know it all." He points out that of course he knew nothing but that the patient needs a rapport "born of ignorance" from the therapist.

This patient would lean against the wall and he could sense that she was getting to the point of "boiling over". When he thought that she was near this he would let her touch his books or move around the room, but still within the bounds that he felt he could tolerate. He also felt free to terminate the session, sometimes after only ten minutes, if he felt that she would boil over or he was too exhausted to hold her through the potential eruption.

> Only touching personalized the space and time for her and made it bearable to be in the analytic situation. This impasse went on for months. In fact, there is a whole impression of her body with the clean smudge of her hands on the wall where she used to stand. It was my capacity to hold her in the analytic space in this way that gradually led to her toleration of me as a separate person, distant but related. I must add that if I found her boiling over, or myself getting exhausted, I would terminate the session after only ten minutes. She could accept that, grudgingly, but she had to be *facilitated* to leave, because separating at the end of the session was acutely traumatic to her. (Khan, 1973, p.237)

In the case of this very disturbed young woman, Khan's ability to tolerate her wild behaviour and set boundaries at the same time enabled her to reach a state in which she could bear his presence and allow herself to speak occasionally. She also could tolerate his verbalising a little of what he thought were the fluctuations of her mood. (Khan, 1973, p. 231-246)

The therapist's own ending

This section will consider the fears of the therapist for her own future as she considers retiring. The areas that will be covered include the anxieties about money and the lack of pensions for many therapists, the lack of identity related to work, and the lack of a community of colleagues. All of these have their own objective validity and are also connected to the past of each therapist. Illustrations will be taken from interviews with therapists who have recently retired or are about to retire.

Fears about ending or retiring are clearly evident in both therapists and their patients. Since such fears are common human phenomena, we can reasonably expect that endings, especially those caused by the therapist, will often be painful and may be difficult to assimilate and accept. Therapists' own personal experience will be involved in the way in which they tolerate the more difficult aspects of analytic work and the anticipation of loss. Klein's paper on "Mourning and manic depressive states" is useful in showing why, in dealing with loss, both therapist and patient are challenged to assume the depressive position.

> Unpleasant experiences and the lack of enjoyable ones in the young child, especially lack of happy and close contact with loved people increase ambivalence, diminish trust and hope and confirm inner anxieties about inner annihilation and external persecution. (Klein, 1940, p. 347)

Some children, she points out, are so dominated by their internal state that even evidence of love or safety from external reality will not be powerful enough to enable the child to process the reality of loss. This helps us to understand the difficulty of an ending caused by the therapist. The good, loved therapist becomes identified with the persecuting object that withdraws love and the patient can no longer feel secure in being loved and kept safe. Klein was an acute and perceptive observer of the fears of the young child. Extrapolating what she observed in the infant and the young child to the adult was partly enabled by Klein's own personal experience.

Klein experienced losses and endings in her own life and we have some idea of what they meant to her from her own unfinished autobiography, and from Phyllis Grosskurth's critical biography. (Grosskurth, 1996) In 1934, Klein had come to England with her children. Her analyst, Karl Abraham, had died just before in 1926 after seeing her for only a year. She was welcomed to London by some analysts, but it was soon after her arrival that her daughter Melitta began to attack her mother, supported by her own analyst, Ernest

Glover. Klein was invited to lecture about her work with children by Ernest Jones, and won some support. Her experience of loss was not left to recover gradually. In 1934, her older son Hans was walking in the mountains when he fell to his death. Melitta said that he had killed himself but there seems no evidence to support this assertion, which seems to have been part of Melitta's hatred of her mother. As we might expect, this loss brought back other losses — her father, her mother, and her sister. (Segal, 2004, p. 14) Klein became depressed but was able to make use of her own experience in her seminal papers on the psychogenesis of manic depressive states. (Klein, 1975) She recognised the element of triumph in mourning, "you have died but I am still alive" which can be followed by the recognition of guilt and the gradual rehabilitation of the good object.

We do not need to examine the lives of the early analysts to discover the effects of loss. Most adults know this from their own experience, and those who become analytic therapists are likely to have been hurt themselves. Why would people who have struggled with loss, facing perhaps their own difficulties with it, willingly face loss by encouraging the ending of analytic work with their patients? With each person who has become an important part of the therapist's life, there will be some sort of mourning process. Klein lost not only family but also friends such as Paula Heimann, who withdrew her support, admiration, and affection and left Klein lonely, if not alone, in London.

In her paper of 1940, Klein pointed out that the response of the child or the adult faced with the loss of the therapist may be to assume an imagined omnipotence:

> Omnipotence however is so closely bound up in the unconscious with the sadistic impulses with which it was first associated that the child feels again and again that his attempts at reparation have not succeeded or will not succeed. His sadistic impulses he feels, may easily get the better of him. (Klein, 1940, p. 350)

The importance of this resort to omnipotence is clear to anyone who has to deal with the distress of patients whose ending of therapy has been painful and counterproductive. The need to be able to triumph over the object which is no longer to be trusted is also part of this process. In complaints processes, we see the wish for triumph and the wish to destroy the treacherous object both experienced and defended against. The hope is that the testing of reality, which can be provided by processes of mediation and reconciliation, might enable the patient to feel that his loved and loving experience with his therapist can still be strong enough to survive hatred and attack.

Klein also saw the importance of achieving an awareness of sadness. The patient who is told by his therapist that the therapy must end will have to overcome all sorts of emotional disturbance, and in some cases may never achieve sadness which implies that hate and destructiveness have diminished:

> Anne was a newly qualified social worker who came to see a therapist, Mrs T, in order to get some help with the stress that she was discovering in the work. She began by saying that she knew she would be difficult. She had been to see a therapist a few years previously and walked out after two sessions. Mrs T immediately felt that she was being challenged to be better than this discarded therapist. Not surprisingly, there was a history in which Anne had experienced the breakup of her parents' marriage when she was five. She could just remember her mother saying "Well. That is the end of that. Now I'm stuck with you." Mrs T was shocked by this and could hardly believe that the mother had meant that she was stuck with Anne. Whether or not the phrase was used historically, it became the theme of the work between the two. Anne used drugs, mostly cocaine, and was given to fits of rage in which she would shout at the therapist, blind and deaf with fury.

> Since Mrs T was working in a clinic, there were other people working in neighbouring rooms and they began to complain about the noise, which was disturbing other vulnerable people. After a while she asked Anne to moderate her volume. Not surprisingly, this had the effect of increasing the rage of Anne, who seemed to feel that Mrs T was prioritising the wellbeing of the other people over her. After a few more weeks, Mrs T decided that she would have to end the work, which seemed to be making Anne more disturbed rather than less. She consulted with a senior member of the profession who said that the patient was abusing the therapy and the therapist, and Mrs T should stop the work. Mrs T was very nervous but told Anne in the next session that she would not be able to continue

and that this would be the last session. Anne was predictably enraged. She shouted her anger and her distress that here was another mother who felt "stuck" with her and she could not bear it. She walked out immediately before Mrs T had a chance to say any more. Mrs T felt a complete failure. She was not able to sustain her own anger and righteous indignation that had enabled her to bring the sessions to an end. She merely felt that she should have been able to contain the agonising rage and distress of the patient.

The next phase was punishment from Anne who attacked Mrs T in several ways. She began by leaving telephone messages threatening to make complaints. This did not seem to be too alarming as Mrs T was confident that she had not behaved unethically, even though she had not been able to achieve the outcome she had wished. This was followed, not by a formal complaint, but a series of telephone calls at all hours of the day and night on Mrs T's home telephone. Anne filled the answerphone with messages, many of which consisted merely of silence that was filled with menace.

Eventually, Mrs T decided that since this piece of her past could not be left behind as it was, she had better see whether she could do any more work. One day, she answered the telephone and found that it was Anne. She found herself offering a meeting to see whether there was anything she could do to help with the feelings that she had engendered in Anne. This offer was accepted and with great misgivings, Mrs T agreed to further sessions. She felt that she had somehow been defeated and that she had avoided, but not managed, what felt like catastrophic anger. Her task was to learn to be less afraid of the patient's anger and more confident of her own strength.

The therapist's fears

Therapists do not generally like foreclosing the work with patients. Any kind of therapist-imposed ending causes anxiety. This section will examine what happens to the patients when therapists tell them of impending endings, whether that is with good notice or more immediate. It will draw on my interviews with retiring therapists. Why does anyone choose to train as a psychotherapist or psychoanalyst? Motivations are as diverse as the people involved, but one or two themes emerge. One major theme is having been helped by psychotherapy when life had become very difficult. This experience is somewhere in the background for many trainee therapists. The next common theme is the belief that listening is helpful and that the candidate is a "good listener". Many candidates applying for training cite their friends' encouragement, either overt or implied, on the basis of being a good listener. Together with the nature of the first career, this ability will certainly contribute to the aptitude that the person has for training. It may or may not, however, be the kind of experience that the training committees are seeking, but it does imply that the candidate will want a career in which relating in some way, however one sided this might be, is going to be important. Some candidates are openly seeking a career which will be worthwhile and will give satisfaction at many levels.

The relevance of this motivation becomes clear when one begins to interrogate the data over questions of therapist attitudes to enabling or accepting endings from their clients. If the therapist has identified herself through her choice of a second career, the need for patients will not be just a matter of financial survival but will constitute identity and possibly self-respect. This is a hypothesis which was put to the test in interviews with psychotherapists facing retirement.

Fears in the consulting room will meld into a mixture which must include the therapist's feelings about losing the dependence, the expectations, and the demands of the patients, as well as the therapist's own personal fears. Some of this will be a relief and some will be a loss. This section will draw on Searle's paper on the loss of the Oedipal love object.(Searle, 1959)

> Julia was a woman who came to see Dr A, a medically qualified psychotherapist. Julia was suffering from MS and was moderately depressed. Her GP had prescribed anti-depressants and some therapeutic work. She did not find any relief from the anti-depressants and settled into some work with the therapist. She was the youngest of a family of four children and said that her childhood had been happy. She could not produce an early memory when asked, but said that she had got on well with both her father and mother "as far as she could remember".. She had various experi-

ences of relationships with men. The last one had ended unhappily with the man simply sending her a text to say that he thought the relationship was "not working" and he would not see her any more. This seemed to be the immediate trigger of the depression, although Dr A was very aware of the physical concomitant which was a serious and debilitating illness leading to death. Dr A did not think that the therapy went well and there were long silences and no sense of any relief.

Trouble arose when Dr A had to take some leave because of a serious flu virus. She was able to let her patients know that she would hope to return in two weeks, but she said that she had flu and that she needed to give herself long enough to recover properly. She fixed a date for the next session and, feeling somewhat better, duly waited for Julia. She did not attend. Dr A also waited for the next weekly session. Still there was no sign of Julia. Dr A began to feel guilty. It was because of her illness that sessions had been missed in the first place. Was this ending caused by her? Alternatively, of course, Julia might be having a serious episode or even have died. The fantasies multiplied and Dr A's guilt began to impinge on her work with other people. She felt that she was inadequate and incompetent, and as she felt so, she gradually became. She found herself forgetting and neglecting those patients that were attending their sessions. She reached a point at which she realised that she needed to return to her own therapy in order to resolve this countertransference.

Searles is very clear that the therapist will have to resolve the countertransference, just as the patient has to reach a point where he can live with the transference. He quotes Edith Weigert: "The analyst is able to treat the analysands on terms of equality; he is no longer needed as an auxiliary superego, an unrealistic deity in the clouds of detached neutrality. There are signs that the patient's labour of mourning for infantile attachments nears completion..." (Searles, 1965, p. 286)

Dr A had to resolve her own difficulties with ending without knowing what went on in her patient's head. She went through several phases in this process. First she was anxious, then guilty. At this point, she was trying to find some power for herself in a situation where she was essentially powerless. If she had caused the ending she might feel bad, but she had not been powerless. As she worked through this stage in her own mind, she had to recognise that she had not deliberately caused the ending, since being ill was not a conscious choice. She then moved into the next phase, which was anger with the patient. She found herself talking to the patient in her head, demanding to know why she had reacted so unreasonably to a few sessions missed for illness.

Dr A's therapist helped her with this anger, which became repetitive. "You might prefer being angry with her to being angry with yourself, but you have already told me that you do not know why she has not returned." This slowly sank in and Dr A began to let the anger go. As the anger receded, it left space for the sadness of lost opportunities. "There might have been more that we could usefully have done, but now we will probably not do any more together." Gradually this too transformed into an ability to be glad about what had been done, which could survive alongside the sadness and memory of the anger. At last, there could be some acknowledgment of a little relief that a difficult patient had simply left and was dealing with her difficulties on her own. This source of guilt took a long time to bring to the surface, and was painful for the conscientious therapist to accept. All of this represents a great deal of work for the therapist to have managed. She could probably have done most of it on her own, but her return to therapy helped her to articulate and clarify the process.

The therapist's desire

This brings us to the recognition of one of the most difficult areas of ending: the therapist's reluctance to accept her own wish for the patient to leave. Even though few in the profession have thoroughly analysed their own reasons for doing the work and are content with the two respectable motives – to earn money and to learn – nevertheless, because of the emphasis in all codes of ethics on patient welfare, the therapist does not wish to give up on the difficult or negative patient. The people with the greatest psychological needs are the people who are most likely to test the therapist's ability to tolerate them in order to discover just how hated and unendurable they are. They are the ones whose parents were not present or could not feel or show any love or attachment. Therapists know that they need to make this experience different, and yet there comes a point where the patient becomes unbearable. Dr A experienced flu, which is a virus infection, not primarily psychosomatic and yet, if she were the patient in this case, we might be looking at the readiness for some sort of somatic compliance. Perhaps she really did not want to go on seeing this patient and that is why she felt so guilty. Joyce McDougall discussed this in relation to ulcers. A patient left when she developed an ulcer, and McDougall considered that illness might sometimes protect a possible victim from being harmed.

> There's a tendency just to say, "I'm sick". But sometimes, when you ask, for example, "Do you have any reason to think that circumstances might have brought this about at this moment? Some time back you felt that your rage and destructiveness were getting out of hand. You've been terribly worried about your marital situation; you've been in deep distress for quite some time. Have you thought that these circumstances might have anything to do with the sudden appearance of the ulcer?" Many patients then give their own theory about their physiological illnesses. And we might by the same token learn quite a lot more about their unconscious fantasy life.
>
> I take the standpoint that the body is communicating something to the patient and that, therefore, if the patient talks to me about a physiological symptom, the patient's body is communicating something to me. Strangely, though, often patients don't mention their illnesses at all, particularly if they think the illnesses have no psychological significance. Sometimes the patients are afraid of being boring, and so they avoid talking about their aches and pains. On the other hand, others talk about their somatic suffering a great deal, frequently because they discovered in childhood that they were important to somebody when they were sick. People with respiratory and skin allergies often say, "Mother was utterly uninterested in our psychological problems. But when we were ill she was always there." The mother is remembered as never having listened to their emotional pain but uniquely interested in their physical suffering. A secondary benefit to be drawn from the sudden explosion of psychosomatic illnesses is that one becomes interesting. (McDougall, 1992, p. 99)

If Dr A is ashamed of her wish to finish working with this patient, then her illness perhaps protected her from this knowledge, although it did not of course protect the patient from whatever it meant to her.

Resolution

The only hope for both of them if they were to avoid this unsatisfactory ending would have been to recognise the difficulties and go back a step. Perhaps Dr A could have begun to consider the rage and disturbance that the patient was keeping quiet. Her evidence for this was only in the ending of the relationship that Julia had mentioned at the beginning. Paying it some attention would have possibly brought to the surface some of the repressed rage that was looking for a place to attach itself on the surface. Staying and facing the full blast of the infant's rage so that it can become possible to think about it is never easy, but it is the therapist's job to try to make it happen if she can.

CHAPTER SIX

Therapy is a manic defence

The previous chapter considered some of the problems with loss leading to the desire to stop the therapy. In this chapter, I shall consider the problems of the therapist who faces her hatred of the patient and her own weariness, leading to her barely acknowledged wish to end the therapy. The therapist who is honest with herself is almost certain to encounter the person whom she sometimes wishes she was not seeing. There are many reasons for this, and it will not always be the same kind of problem that leads to the sinking of the heart when it is time to see a particular person. Each therapist needs to be willing to disentangle the nature of the reasons so that she recognises the extent to which she is responding to the patient's suffering, and to what extent her own pain is being brought to the surface by the case.

The therapist wishes to end her own suffering

One of the first and most obvious considerations is the weariness and unwillingness to face anger, frustration, and pain again. The therapist grows old and tired, both literally and metaphorically, and should accept that this may need to be recognised. Psychoanalysis is a discipline which has paid considerable attention to human development and the processes by which the newly conceived embryo becomes a fully functioning adult, and all the vicissitudes on the way. Looking at the main texts on human psychological development, we can see that the bulk of the developmental theory relates to childhood. Gordon Lowe (Lowe, 1972) in his book on development spends no more than pages 243 to 257 on old age, which he defines as extending from age sixty-five onwards. He points out that old age is relative, and that few people think of themselves as old until they are in their eighties or nineties, when he considers that it becomes unavoidable to do so. He points out that the relativity saves younger old people from recognising their position because there may still be people they know who are older or sicker. Such old people may scrutinise the obituary columns in order to check that the people dying are older than they are. If they are not older, they died before their time. Katherine Whitehorn, in a *Point of View* broadcast in 2013 on BBC Radio 4, raised an objection to the general avoidance of the use of the word "old" which means that most people prefer to talk about "older" people, so emphasising the relative.

What is clear is that old age is difficult to accept, both for those who have reached it and for those who look at it and understand that they will get there some day. Getting old involves all sorts of losses and the necessary defences against them. These are the focus of analytic work because although some of them are helpful and even necessary, some of them are painful and work against us.

Work as a manic defence

A manic defence, in Klein's view, would be whatever thinking or behaviour protects against the recognition of loss. Such defences operate to kill or destroy the parents so that they cannot injure the patient or be a danger to each other. This applies to all the internal objects. They all have to be mastered and controlled so that they cannot do any harm. There is a hunger for objects to control, and the root of this need lies in the fear that the parents will have intercourse and produce another child. (Klein, 1975, p. 278) This is relevant to the therapist, who is thinking of ending work with one patient or with all of them in retirement. She needs to keep the children with her so that she can control them and her own feelings.

Some of the anxieties that will be considered relate to being super-seded by the next generation. Much of the anxiety is about imposing an ending on the patients who will then become hostile, or even just bereft. In either case, the relationship of love and admiration which may never have been achieved as much as the therapist hoped, is no longer something that can be hoped for next week or the week after. It has to be given up. All of these losses, both of people and of inter-nal objects, have to be faced by the therapist who is thinking of end-ing work, and the effort gives rise to manic defences which might often take the form of more work.

Manic defences

Klein also points out that the superego is involved in the processes that we all endure. (Ibid.) The depressive position involves recognis-ing guilt and sorrow for phantasised attacks on the loved mother, her care, attention, and food. This guilt and sorrow is difficult to endure and leads to the omnipotent manic defence in which we do not have to endure these painful feelings. At a conscious, level some of these ideas will be familiar to all therapists. No-one can escape the understanding that she has not always been as helpful to any patient as she might wish. Sometimes she has been tired or ill or just lazy. Sometimes she has not understood what she was told. In any case, there have been failings. The guilt and sorrow for these failings are painful to accept, and in themselves are likely to induce manic om-nipotence, which can allow a belief that those painful feelings will never occur again. Ironically, the therapist in this position is likely to take on more patients in the constant search for the work that will justify the whole endeavour.

The idea that activities that we love could be diminished in some way by calling them "defences" is disturbing to some therapists. Per-haps we need to arrive at a moderate position in which activities can still be loved for their own sake, and yet can also be recognised to be serving a defensive function. On the other hand, if all of life is a de-fence against death, there is no longer any meaning in the work. The only point in saying that work is a defence against thoughts of death would be to say that work at a certain stage of life becomes a particularly useful defence against those thoughts. Recognising this might lead to considering the value of work. Is it the appropriate satisfaction for the stage of life that has been reached? It is a reminder that we might benefit from facing the hidden thought.

For some therapists, working with patients provides a manic defence protecting them from recognising that their own feelings on growing old need to be recognised and faced. Michael Jacobs in *The Presenting Past* describes the possibility of ego integrity, taking this well beyond the integrity visualised by Erik Erikson (Erikson, 1965) in his eighth stage of human life. Gordon Lowe's description of depression in old age might apply to the therapist who is anxious that she has not achieved as much as she had originally hoped with her patient:

> The feeling of despair may be hidden by an apparent disgust with life as an almost somatic revulsion at years not used but merely spent or containing too many disappointments and disillusionments so that a satisfactory culmination in old age has become impossible. (Jacobs, 2005, p. 257)

This description might apply to a therapist with a patient who is not making changes but seems to be still depressed and wretched. The time with the patient may seem to have been spent rather than used, even though there is an argument that any time given to the patient, with all his own misery, is time that the patient can make useful for himself. It is time that no-one else will bother to spend with someone who is full of depressive rumination. Any such consideration is likely to be rejected by the therapist, whose countertransference is in itself depressive and unable to hear or use any consolation. She will not be willing to let herself off this hook, but will need to work with herself as she would with a depressed patient.

The therapist must ask herself about her own anger. She might press a patient to discover the person with whom he is really angry. When she asks herself this question she will unearth her own transference to the patient. Few writers have gone into depth about this area but it would be difficult to believe that the therapist is exempt from the universal human tendency to impose patterns from the past on the people who are encountered in the present.

A therapist, Mrs G, was seeing a patient, Alice, aged 87, who had been sent by her son. The son, Gerald, had rung Mrs G and said that his mother was a strong, independent woman who had recently become depressed and seemed to have lost interest in looking after herself. She had begun to neglect her house, not cleaning as she always had before, and not cooking for herself. Gerald said that he had arranged for an agency to send someone each day to make a meal for her and check that she was all right. She would not allow these carers to clean and became very angry if they said that things needed doing that she had ignored. All of this was very distressing for her son because his mother had been the Head Mistress of a large comprehensive school, and was interested in art and music and was capable of completing *The Times* crossword in about ten minutes.

Mrs G decided that she would ignore the analytic belief that it is difficult to work with anyone over 40, and would take on her first elderly patient. Alice was cautious and unwilling to talk at first but she came to each session in a taxi and since she had a regular booking, the taxi brought her faithfully week after week. It became routine and she relaxed and began to talk more freely. Mrs G thought that she was helpful and was pleased with the work. Unfortunately, Alice began a descent into forgetfulness. She began to telephone several times to check whether she really had an appointment. She also forgot what had been said. At first she forgot only what had been said the previous week, but after a while she showed signs of forgetting what was said a few minutes before. Mrs G was able to help her to understand her fear of being useless to her clever son. She seemed to accept that she might be able to allow him to help her now, just as she had looked after him when he was small. Mrs G pointed out that this was a natural and inevitable process. Alice seemed to accept this but she would repeat the same thought seven times before she left, and the same thing the next week, and gradually began to revert to the same plaintive mantra no matter what had been said.

Mrs G began to find herself getting angry and impatient. She imagined telephoning Gerald and saying that working with his mother was no longer useful. She convinced herself that this was the only ethical option as he was paying for his mother to have therapy. Before she did this, she decided that she would consult a supervisor. The supervisor understood but was not in agreement with the plan. He said that perhaps Mrs G wanted to get away from the recognition of the descent of someone who had begun as an educated and competent woman into a state of senility bordering on dementia. This made sense and Mrs G began to feel very sad and regretful. She had not been able to help Alice enough when she was still able to hear and absorb what was said to her. These feelings buried the anger and left her wanting to end the therapy by any possible means. She began to consider telling Gerald to get his mother into the psychiatric services, although she knew that these resources were unlikely to offer any kind of talking therapy. She convinced herself that this would be all right because Alice was no longer able to use it. Again she met with the supervisor who asked her to consider her own reluctance to the minimal nature of what could be achieved with Alice. Nevertheless, he said, that minimal change may be important to her. How do you know that she is not better off with her one hour a week with you than if everyone gives up on her? Mrs G began to think seriously about her own life. She was sixtythree and was aware that she had avoided considering the need for her own retirement to be planned within the next five to ten years. She decided that she would stop taking on new patients in three years and would retire before she was seventy. She was not at all sure that she would be ready to retire and still felt very shaky about what it would mean. She recognised that one of her main fears was that she would be like Alice, distinctly and recognisably old.

Mrs G was wise and decided that her own feelings were in such a state of flux that she had better find a therapist for herself. Her dilemma then was to consider what sort of therapist she would be able to tell this difficulty to. If she found someone older than her, he might understand her dilemma but it might impact on him just as her own relationship with Alice had bothered her. If it were someone younger, how would he know what it felt like to be faced with old age and all the losses that it might involve? What if she asked a therapist whether he wanted to work with this question? She found someone who simply said, "These are questions that we all have to face if we live long enough. I don't know the answers but I believe it is important to ask the questions." She decided to try to work on this with the person who saw the value of the questions. Of course, he did not tell her how old he was but he looked to her to be about her own age, and she guessed that the questions were quite real to him.

In her own therapy, Mrs G began to talk about her fear of all sorts of losses when she retired. She remembered that her own mother's death had been unexpected and had happened when she was only sixty-five. This had seemed a tragedy at the time, and yet friends and colleagues all said how good it was that she had died quickly and had not suffered. Mrs G began to realise that although this was true, she was angry with her mother for leaving her so suddenly and not showing her how to deal with old age and decline. This anger had been repressed because she had been very sad to lose her mother and had cried a great deal on her own. Gradually, she recognised that her anger with Alice had something to do with resentment that this woman was still alive and, however inadequately, was available to her son.

This story illustrates one of the infinite number of ways in which the therapist's own experience will interact with the problems brought by the patients.

Patient complaints

On the whole, the profession does not show good models of ending. One of the most shocking experiences of sitting on one of the central ethics committees in the UK in the early twenty-first century has been the number of highly experienced and conscientious therapists about whom complaints have been made because of some difficulty with ending. Not all of them are concerned with the internal processes of the therapists. Recent examples, however, have shown that this has always played some part, and that part can appear under the stress of a complaint hearing, even though in the consulting room the therapist is able to keep it to herself. Clearly it is inappropriate to write about the details of anyone's hearing, both for the sake of the patient and the therapist concerned. On the other hand, the principles at stake need to be considered by us all. *Nihil humani a me alienum* ("nothing human is alien from me", usually ascribed to the Latin historian,

Terence).

Several problems have arisen because the therapist was unwilling to allow an ending. Several others have come about through the pain of the patient who felt pushed out by a therapist who had changed, or who was unwilling to be the idealised object that the patient wanted. A fictional account can illustrate the difficulties of the therapist with a particular presentation by a patient:

> Mr Y was practising as a therapist. He was sixty and was beginning to think that he might retire soon. His partner had died five years before, and he felt that work was important to keep him alert. He had deliberately taken his work to a supervisor to ensure that his own mourning had not interfered too much with his work. His supervisor had said that Mr Y's own personal grief seemed to have deepened and enhanced the work. He had not seen any problem. The patient who complained was James, a man of forty-three, who had come with problems as a gay man suffering from an inability to make relationships last beyond a brief encounter for sex.

> James had discovered that he was able to continue in therapy beyond a brief encounter, and this filled him with hope and joy. He not only loved his therapist, but fell in love with him too. He found it difficult to speak about this and conveyed the strength of his feeling only by sitting gazing at his therapist, and by his reluctance to leave at the end of sessions. This was difficult for Mr Y, who felt that James's feelings were demanding something more of him than he was prepared to give. He refrained from any kind of recognition of the feelings but found himself being more brisk than usual. One day at the end of a session when James was simply sitting still after Mr Y had said "it's time", he lost his temper. "There are other people waiting you know. You are not the only person I have to see." In telling his supervisor this, he was aware that he might have sounded angry "because", he acknowledged, "I really was furious with him. I'm not sure why I was so angry."

> This admission was enough to make Mr Y pause and consider what was going on, but before he had been able to analyse his feelings he received an e-mail from James. The e-mail said that he was very angry and would not be attending sessions any more. It was clear, it said, that other people were more important to Mr Y than James, and that made the therapy useless. Mr Y was very upset by this. He

immediately referred it to his lost partner in his own mind and was very angry with James for intruding on his grief. In fact, James was reacting in an understandable way to being unloved. Mr Y sent a hasty e-mail saying that he expected James to attend his next session as usual so that they could discuss this situation. He added that he thought there were some important matters in relation to James's father that needed to be discussed. James immediately put in a complaint alleging unprofessional and incompetent behaviour, both for ending the therapy by his behaviour, and for making an interpretation in an e-mail which could not be worked on, and which might not be sufficiently private.

This complaint showed the breakdown of a therapeutic relationship that seems to have been caused, or at least exacerbated, by the therapist's personal circumstances. Having so recently lost his own partner, it was never a good idea for Mr Y to work with a gay man who wanted a stable relationship. The task of the regulating body in this situation is to see whether the therapist can be helped to get back his analytic stance, or whether it is impossible. Some sort of mediation or conciliation meeting would be ideal, and in some cases can be offered. Of course, its efficacy depends on the patient's wish for help exceeding his wish for revenge. There is no one to work with the patient on his wish for revenge, no one to help him consider who is the object of this rage apart from the therapist. In other words, whom does she represent? Unless the patient finds his way to another therapist who will work responsibly with this process, there is unlikely to be any improvement and both he and the therapist will have to suffer right through the whole complaint process.

So what does mourning mean for a therapist and her patients? What was it that made Mr Y unable to work in the usual way with a patient who loved him? Clearly to understand the individual problem requires that we have the information that would normally be available only to the therapist. What was the nature of the object that had cast its shadow on the psyche of Mr Y? If his own partner had, for example, been elusive and difficult to pin down, going out on his own, perhaps pursuing sex in saunas or gay bars on his own, would that have left a residue of anger that attached itself to the patient who did not want Mr Y to go? Of course he was not literally going, but he was requiring an absence. As Matte Blanco points out, the unconscious is not concerned with the order of the terms. You do this to me is the same as I do this to you. (Blanco, 1988, p. 85)

Therapists often find it difficult to tolerate the ways in which their patients are receiving something that they want themselves. In Mr Y's head, there was something going on along the lines of "You've had fifty minutes of my full attention but now you have to accept that it's the end for today." This anger can arise both from the therapist's own deprivation and also from the loss of something that was good. So even if his relationship with his lost partner had been satisfying, he was likely to resent the satisfaction that his patient might have. This seems to imply that there was no hope but that, either way, the patient would have given rise to a countertransference of some difficulty. This may be so, but in any case, the onus is on the therapist to understand it and to make use of it, not to act it out. This is a counsel of perfection and we all need to have empathy and sympathy with the therapist who finds this too difficult to manage. Empathy is important but does not excuse incompetent practice.

Could there have been a constructive ending with this patient? Sadly, the best solution would probably have been not to take him on in the first place. Even though this was likely to go wrong, the therapist found himself in a process which was arousing strong feelings in him. He had the obligation to try to use his experience for the benefit of the patient. If he could not continue to do that, he should have considered the way in which he could end the work. Unlike Khan, (Chapter Four) he might have found it difficult just to end the therapy without any reason given. What reason would be helpful and honest to the patient? Perhaps simply to say that he was not able to provide what he thought James needed, and that he should find another therapist, was as close to his own reality as he would have been able to go. Yet this might have seemed tragic to James, who had already made a powerful and loving transference to Mr Y. On the other hand, if Mr Y could have convinced James that he genuinely cared for his best interests, he might have managed to join in the sadness of the abstinence of a therapeutic relationship. Both of them would have had to lose, as Mr Y already had.

Jung described a case in which he felt he should end:

The whole case worried me so much that I told the patient that there was no sense in her coming to see me for treatment. I didn't understand two thirds of her dreams to say nothing of her symptoms....I had no notion of how I could help her. She looked at me in astonishment and said: "But it is going splendidly! It doesn't matter that I don't understand my dreams. I always have the craziest symptoms but something is happening all the time." (Jung, 1954, p. 334)

The therapist may provide something valuable by remaining available, and perhaps the experience that has formed her may contribute as much to that as to an understanding that can be put into words.

Is it part of the therapist's task to use her own experience to that extent? Many therapists would not use their own experience overtly with a patient. We have all had to spend some time mastering the desire to say "I know all about that, the same thing happened to me..." We know that such personal exposure can lead to the kind of difficulty that Sandor Ferenczi encountered when he tried to do mutual analysis with his patients. He found that he could not continue to be so open, partly because it risked compromising his patients' confidentiality, and partly because it did not make his patients safe enough. On the other hand, most therapists have let something of their own experience creep into their understanding. (Ferenczi, 1991) Without actually saying anything, the therapist shows that, for instance, grief is something that she recognises. Ann Orbach thinks that this is more likely to happen within the Jungian model of therapy than in the Freudian:

And here I think the Jungian view of transference might be more helpful than the Freudian. Instead of being expected to cope with the therapist's almost total anonymity - and for the therapist to have to cope with wearing that anonymous mask - the patient encounters someone who is prepared at least on an unconscious level to share his or her deepest experience of being human so that from the ensuing mix-up something new may be born. (Orbach, 1996, p. 49)

This seems to be a reference to the Jungian metaphor of the search for the way of turning base metals into gold. In order to achieve this, the alchemists heated elements and watched them mingle to form a new compound. This, at least, we can see happening in the therapeutic process.

The aging therapist

While older therapists may contribute to the therapy of their older patients from the wealth of their experience, they also have to consider the realities of old age. Since old age is a relative concept and proceeds at different paces, no-one has legislated for the retirement of therapists. They have to think for themselves about the small losses that might begin to impinge on their ability to do the work effectively. Since listening is the main requirement for a therapist, encroaching deafness is a potential problem that might not be easy to recognise. Since many people find it difficult to accept that they might benefit from a hearing aid, there is no reason to think that therapists will be any better at this, especially as it is a professional necessity that they can hear. Accepting that the patients are not all mumbling but the acuity of hearing is lost will be difficult but is essential.

Losing vision is relevant but perhaps less vital. We depend on visual clues to a greater extent than we consciously know, and much of that awareness of body language will be lost if eye sight is seriously diminished by cataract for example. Most people will have to get cataracts treated and may suffer more from loss of near sight and reading comfort which has less direct impact on patients. Probably the most difficult change for the aging therapist is the loss of mental agility. A normal change that takes place from about sixty onwards is the difficulty in remembering names. Many people worry about their forgetfulness and might joke about it to colleagues. The anxiety is expressed in such phrases as "a senior moment", which conveys that it is common but also that it arouses anxiety. How do I know whether my occasional forgetting of a name or a word is the beginning of a serious dementia, and when it is just part of the normal aging process?

Whatever the case for an individual, any therapist must monitor the extent to which she finds herself forgetting words that she needs for an interpretation. Worse still, she may find herself struggling to remember what she has been told, perhaps by the patient, perhaps by her supervisor. Wilfred Bion's maxim of approaching a session without memory and without desire becomes a source of comfort. (Bion, 1967) Setting aside an anxious striving after facts is one thing, but not being able to remember what happened in the previous session is another.

Bion was clear about what he meant and gives the reasons for it:

> The first point is for the analyst to impose on himself a positive discipline of eschewing memory and desire. I do not mean that "forgetting" is enough: what is required is a positive act of refraining. (Bion, 1970, p. 31)

Bion makes clear that what he is asking for is not forgetting at all, but a refraining from the use of memory or desire. His position requires the therapist to recognize what she remembers and desires for the patient from memory and desire. Bion's concern was that the therapist should help the patient to search for the truth. This, in Bion's terms, is a complex concept of the "ultimate reality" and the ineffable, which he encapsulates as "O". The therapist's task is to help the patient go beyond what he can know from sensory sources, and progress to a position from which he can recognise the intersection of his ordinary knowledge and truth with a deeper awareness. This is what Bion calls the intersection with "O".

The therapist cannot manage without her memory. She needs to be able to suspend the use of it so that something of "ultimate reality" or "O" can begin to appear. Bion gives more detail about why memory might be misleading. He is not at any point saying that the therapist does not need it. Memory is always misleading as a record of fact since it is distorted by the influence of unconscious forces. Desires interfere, by absence of mind when observation is essential, with the operation of judgment. Desires distort judgment by the selection and suppression of the material to be judged. (Bion, 1967, p. 1) The aging therapist might have difficulty with memory as well as with her senses. She might have a more pervasive difficulty which is concerned with resilience and endurance. To the outsider, the physical work of the psychotherapist might seem untaxing to say the least.

Those who do this work know that sitting very still and upright for six or seven hours a day is not as easy as it sounds. Some patients require the therapist to understand that sense of weariness or dullness that can even go as far as sleepiness. The older therapist has to work with this and understand it like any other therapist, but may have more difficulty in distinguishing her own tiredness, and even sleepiness, from something that is induced by the patient and his material. That distinction can usually be made by the therapist who is willing to be honest with a supervisor or consultant.

More difficult perhaps is the general weariness which leads a working therapist to feel that she no longer wants to get up early, or subject herself to listening intently for fifty minutes. Every therapist is liable to short periods of this kind of weariness which usually means that it is time for a holiday. On the other hand, if it persists after a holiday, the therapist has the duty to think that maybe she should consider retiring. This is painful and difficult for many therapists. One interview shows this:

> Another reason that I wanted to retire, and would have needed to wind down, even if I had not been moving, is that I had begun to notice that I could no longer always hold on to a complex argument or train of thought; I noticed this in committee work and also occasionally in clinical work.

This therapist noted her own change and had the courage to come to a decision without external pressure.

In another case, the therapist noted a dysfunctional context which she felt powerless to change:

> One other more controversial, but crucial aspect which led to my decision to retire is attached to the frustration and weariness I felt in the organisation in which I worked, and to what I perceived as its fear of applying psychodynamic understanding to itself as a living, breathing "body". Having worked in various groups over many years, I am struck again and again by the huge anxiety that exists around exploring difference and controversy in the group. Fear of anger and of loss seems frequently to dominate proceedings, preventing work and re-vision. Without Bion's thinking on this I would be at a loss to explain why "elephants in the room" are

frequently left to roam around, stampeding both thought and feeling. I need to exercise some caution here, having learnt from recent lectures and courses that I am in danger of taking the moral high ground. I'm aware too that I need to consider how I found myself in such a group in the first place (but that's another story!). On reflection it seems to me that the pressing, mostly unconscious, needs of each individual continually outweigh the need to form a healthy living and suffering group. Group work can be a very useful resource for the retiring therapist.

This therapist was considering the reasons for retirement from an agency. The reasons were not overtly concerned with any kind of aging in the therapist, and it is perhaps unfair to link them to that, except that she seems to have reached a point at which she could disengage and consider it too big for her to tackle. This may well be the objective reality, but we might note that younger people will often take on impossible tasks and hopeless odds where older people might have a better idea about what is practical.

Some therapists consider the possibility of ending before they make up their minds to retire based on an awareness that sooner or later they will lose their physical strength and ability:

Generally I hope to feel "lighter" and less anxious and I hope to get to know my partner in a new way as we come face to face with new roles in life. I hope to make the most of life while we are still reasonably fit. I do not want to look back with too much regret because I lacked the courage to engage in new ways of being. I do expect to come across the same group difficulties I have always experienced.

Serious ethical concerns may lead to a decision to retire. Therapists have to balance their own understanding of their fitness to practise and weigh that against their agreement to work with the patient. At this point, they will recognise the importance of not saying that the ending will be exclusively under the control of the patient. Some therapists might be tempted to say this at the beginning but will realise that they must maintain their own freedom to end when they feel that they should. In any case, ethical codes require that all endings are undertaken with the wellbeing of the patient in mind. This may not be easy for the therapist, who will miss the opportunity to be told more of a person's intimate and personal story. The patients will also find these endings painful, but may derive something valuable from the honesty and strength of the therapist who does what she knows is in their best interests, even though it hurts everyone.

> I have had two periods of quite serious illness when I was not able to see my patients for several months. This made me very concerned, and I realised that as we get older we are more likely to be ill and I did not want to put my patients at this degree of risk. Very sadly then I decided that I should give them a long period of notice, actually two years. I told them that I was not confident about my health and that I had decided to retire. This made two in particular very unhappy because they had been in therapy with me for a long time. I found their sadness and distress very difficult to bear. They both found other forms of therapy and gradually were able to move on.

> My expectation of retirement was that I would be able to take on short term work of some sort so that I could continue to practise the work that I love. I have found it a great privilege to be able to witness a person's spiritual progress from such close quarters. I miss that greatly and have not yet been able to find an appropriate opportunity to work, even as a volunteer.

This therapist was finding that she had to manage without the help of the manic defence that, at times, can save any of us from the pain of loss. A little work may be possible for a therapist, and may help to delay the time at which the lack of work leaves the therapist to find what she has in her own resources.

This may seem an unduly self-centred approach to the question of whether to continue working. The truth is that the welfare of patients inscribed in all reputable codes of ethics must always be paramount. The therapist must give up her manic defence if she has any reason to think that she is no longer helpful to her patients. On the other hand, she must also consider her own wellbeing, knowing that this is not different from the wellbeing of her patients. A weary or physically ailing therapist is not likely to be good enough. On the other hand a person of advanced years has a wealth of experience, and maybe some of that indefinable quality of wisdom which her patients can see and feel, will perhaps hope to emulate.

CHAPTER SEVEN

Hopes and desires

What did the patient want?

Regardless of the patient's earliest protestations that he wants to change, what he really hopes to find is some ease from the suffering of his symptoms. He also wants some affirmation of his view of himself and the world. Castelnuovo-Tedesco believes that the problem for the therapist throughout the work is the complexity and ambiguity of desire. We might begin with the statement made at assessment about what the patient wants, but we know that only the transference will reveal more than the conscious desires accepted by the ego and permitted by the superego.

> The patient, for his part, responds to the therapist with a range of behaviors traditionally described as resistance, i.e., by balancing "change" with efforts to maintain the status quo. Resistance typically manifests itself as soon as it becomes apparent to the patient that treatment (and, certainly, cure) will involve both more and less than he had anticipated. The "less" part refers to his discovery that he will receive less direct gratification than unconsciously he has sought and expected; the "more" part refers to the realization that

> inevitably some modification of his personal attitudes is called for. (Castelnuovo-Tedesco, 1986, p. 272)

If we think in terms of what patients know that they want, the full extent of desire and demand remain elusive. The famous question posed by writers in English from Geoffrey Chaucer onwards has been, "What does the woman want?" The Wife of Bath's answer that Chaucer gives her so fittingly is "the maistrie" (obsolete form of "mastery"). Human infants also need to have power over their surroundings to the extent that they can extract enough nourishment and support to survive extremely long periods of dependence. Our brains are too big to enable us to be born at a stage of development when we can walk and fend for ourselves. As a result, we experience total dependence that gradually reduces to partial dependence, but remains as social and cultural weakness for fifteen to twenty years. There is no cause for surprise in discovering that most of us put considerable effort into establishing the areas in which we can feel independent, no longer helpless.

As a result of this wish to feel autonomous patients have a fundamental ambivalence when they consult therapists. They want to become powerful and self-determining, but they are putting themselves in the hands of one who is "supposed to know". The therapist must know enough to understand something of the transference of desire and demand in order to help her patient free himself to move within it. The patient's demand that the therapist is the "subject who is supposed to know" is transference of an image of the parent. The therapist is supposed to take responsibility. If the therapist interprets this transference too soon, she will confirm the image of the one who knows. Even not answering questions is a position which can reinforce this illusion: the therapist could produce the answers and so she does know. If the therapist is genuinely convinced, following Freud, that the patient knows the answers himself, both of them can gradually begin to address the question of who will take the authority. The process of clarifying the authority in the consulting room is often crucial to the process of change. This is liable to be difficult, as each person seeks to avoid responsibility. That is appropriate for the therapist, but a symptom for the patient.

Investigating the therapist

The first phase of therapy is likely to be taken up with skirmishes while the patient tries to establish a picture of the person whom he is addressing. He wants to know what sort of desire he can impute to this therapist. This is most obvious in the case of someone who has been abused in some way:

> Luis is a man who has described his mother as intrusive and inappropriate with him. She would find reasons to burst in on him in the bathroom when he was fifteen or sixteen, and she treated his bedroom as a place to sit and smoke. He was very quiet and tentative with his female therapist, Mrs B, until one day he told her how frightened he was because he had day dreams in which she figured. When he summoned up the courage to tell her a bit more, it was that he was afraid that she wanted sex with him. This could be a way of hiding his own desire for her from himself, but Mrs B thought that he was also anxious to discover whether she wanted to overwhelm him and take away his inadequate penis. The young boy being looked at by his mother was still there in some sense.

This situation is difficult for any therapist. The patient, now an adult man, both wants her to want him, and wants to be safe to have the childhood that he missed. His unconscious does not know what is important. Of course, there is nothing for the therapist to do other than articulate the dilemma. This is difficult because it makes explicit the sexual tension with the therapist, and if it is too early the patient may flee, misinterpreting the statement as an expression of desire. The patient at this point is in danger of believing that ending the therapy is the only way to bring peace. Such a view of the ending as the solution to a problem is inherent in therapy, with the abused in particular, but not only with them. The therapy can be made into the focus of the pain that can then be avoided. This is not a fruitful course for the patient as the relief that may be experienced by leaving is based on the illusory nature of the transference.

The power of the desire of the abuser means that the abused person is likely to transfer patterns in which the powerful person asks too much. This can apply whether or not the projection is aimed at someone the patient experiences as benevolent. Levy and Young emphasise the frequency of this form of transference for abused patients:

> It is important to recognise however, that in the mind of the pa-
> tient, particularly a patient with a history of abuse, a potent thera-
> pist can be experienced as dangerous and destructive. (Levy &
> Young, 2004, p. 131)

These writers go on to consider Caroline Garland's theoretical discussion of the reasons why this kind of work is likely to come to a
fruitless ending. She points out that survivors of abuse may be suffering from an interruption of their capacity to think symbolically.
They are unable to process experiences through symbols. They may
be trapped in a process of repetition that does not get modified unless there is skilled intervention. Levy and Young refer to Freud's
account of the child who managed his distress at his mother's absence by hiding the cotton reel and playing the "*fort da* game". This
small child would hide the cotton reel saying "*fort*" in German, which
means "away" or "gone". He would then find it and say "*da*", reassuring himself that what is lost can be found and that he can take
control of it. This process illustrates the wish to identify with the
aggressor, in other words, to become the mother leaving and throwing away her little boy, not the little boy being left. This might make
us think about the possibility of the patient throwing away the therapist who has held the power to give or not give, to stay or go. (Ibid, p.
132)

What kind of love?

Even if this were a way to achieve the sense of relief at the lack of
impingement or interference, we might consider that a rather minimal achievement. Yet for many people, peace is anything but minimal. The main world religions all have something to say about peace.
The Christian religious perspective places peace as the highest good:
one prayer is that the dead may rest in peace (*requiescant in pace*), but
peace is not only for the dead. "Peace I leave with you, my peace I
give unto you. Not as the world giveth give I unto you." (*Gospel according to John*, Ch. 24, v. 27) A search for peace of mind might be one
aim of therapeutic work. It might be a description of the acknowledged

purpose of remembering in order to forget. Patients are tormented by memories. Obviously memories are part of the patient's life story and cannot be taken away. Fortunately, the impact that they have in the present can be modified. Peace that is useful to the patient can be found in living with the trauma in the past, not cutting it out of experience like therapeutic surgery.

Patients might have other hopes. Those who have experienced some sort of sexual abuse or who, as Freud came to believe, have experienced the wish for sexual or at least erotic satisfaction from the parent of the opposite sex, may have hopes that relate to some sort of seduction. Most therapists will experience at some stage in their career, the heat of an erotic demand from a patient, often (but not always) of the opposite sex. Because this is known to be predictable but unacceptable, in practice it will be very often hidden in the twists and turns of the imagery and the subtle tones of the material that the patient brings. The therapist *should* find this difficult to bring into consciousness, even when she recognises it.

There are more than the usual questions about appropriate timing. Bringing erotic desire into consciousness and into the space between the two people in the consulting room is very likely to arouse either shame or aggressive demand. If it is shame, the patient may seek relief in absence. This may be one of the main reasons for unannounced departures. A therapist who has just made an interpretation about erotic desire might expect that there will be some sort of response, and would not be entirely surprised by absence. In fact, the therapist might be slightly relieved if the patient does not reappear at the next session.

Experience is very helpful in this area and enables the therapist to overcome her own shame at talking about sexuality and erotic fantasies with the patient. A helpful training supervisor is also of great value in that she will normalise the erotic element in the patient's experience. The most valuable learning is, of course, the experience of desire in the personal analysis. The training analyst has a particular responsibility to pick up this desire because she needs to enable the therapist to understand the importance and ubiquity of desire, and not only to understand it but to enable the patient to address it. So what is it that the therapist and the patient need to address? In a tribute to Jean Laplanche, Susan Heenan-Wolff writes of Jacques Lacan's view of the way in which the parents introduce the infant and child to sexuality. It should not be through an experience of abuse but through the normal handling and control of the body, which is bound to be affected by an attitude to the infant's physical existence.

> Sexuality is implanted in the child by the adult… The child is exposed to these messages. It is able to translate for itself in part but in part not. These untranslated parts are the building blocks of the emerging unconscious. (Heenan-Wolff, 2013, p. 437)

If the therapist's acknowledgement of the infant's physical existence in the adult is tolerant and accepting, with a degree of warmth, then the patient, who is unconsciously associating this experience with his infantile handling may feel some hope for a satisfaction that belongs to infancy. The adult may expect a state of bliss. This is a hope in most people; from some it may be a demand. If the therapist is not aware of this, she may be puzzled by the level of frustration and disappointment about an outcome which has not been formulated. Sometimes this sort of ending is angry. More often it is simply represented by an absence which leaves frustration and disappointment behind it.

The problem might be in divergent views of the nature and purpose of therapy. If, as Levy and Young state, the value of therapy is in helping people to face and mourn losses, then hope is not the point. The patient must face the loss of the pre-traumatic self, not just of the people or things that we all lose as we progress through life stages. They state that any therapeutic work must involve mourning:

> Much of it is in the domain of mourning a series of losses, essentially of the pre-trauma self but also resurrected losses of the life one longed to have had, the parents one wished to have had, the lost circumstances, the lost opportunities. (Levy & Young, 2004, p. 137)

The therapist may be tempted to identify with the non-protecting parent. This parent might have been irritated or angry with the victim state of the child. This aspect of the relationship may get re-enacted in the transference, making it difficult for the therapist to maintain a stance of neutrality with the patient, who is stuck in the least productive stage of mourning. The resentful feelings of the child may be projected onto the people who are encountered in everyday life, allowing the adult to feel like a perpetual victim. The therapist, fortunately, will have the experience of those who receive the projections. She will then be able to deal with her reaction by putting it into words for herself, and by understanding the reason for it so that something of this reality may be communicated to the patient, if that could be helpful.

The implication is that the work of therapy is to lead to different hopes. The patient will perhaps be able to stop trying to convert everyone into a persecutor. This would not be a conscious hope but becomes a powerful pattern which is difficult to change.

> Joan came to see a therapist because she had vivid dreams and her friend had told her that she should get a therapist to tell her what they meant. Mrs N was an experienced psychodynamic counsellor but found herself unable to say very much to this client, and when she asked herself why she was limited in this way, she realised that she was afraid of hurting the client, who would probably get very angry. Mrs N had to reach the understanding that the transference that was required involved a scenario in which Joan was the victim of a bullying, overbearing parent. Joan had told very little of her history, saying only that her childhood was "fine" with no big difficulties.
>
> Mrs N had to risk a construction of a past in which someone had managed to be too powerful and overbearing, but perhaps in a way which other people would not have noticed. Joan said nothing directly, but brought a dream to the next session in which she and her younger sister were riding bicycles along a narrow path with a steep drop on each side. Suddenly a man appears on the path in front and they both try to avoid him and fall off the path. Her sister is lying in a crumpled heap at the bottom while she lands on a shelf of rock and is not hurt. Joan's own associations to this are that her Dad was always in the way and she and her sister would always try to avoid him. At this point, she stopped talking and would not take her associations any further. Mrs N went on thinking about the dangerous nature of this blockage which killed her sister in the dream. She also thought about the transference implications of herself as the person who blocked the client from moving forward. She

knew that she was the chief hope for moving forward without disaster, but she also represented the fear of disaster if the past were acknowledged. There was also the wish that the sister would be the one who was destroyed, leaving Joan herself to observe from a safe, if uncomfortable, place.

Over time, Mrs N was able to begin helping Joan to see that some of her fears were expressed in this dream, and that out of these fears some new hopes could develop. Specifically in this case, Joan was able to hope that she could cycle on a path where she would not be at such risk, and where her father or anyone else could stand on the path and not cause an accident. She spent another year developing her possibility for making choices that did not involve making another person into an enemy.

Clearly this condensed account cannot show how understanding came and went, and how many setbacks were surmounted in the process. What it does show is that an unhappy ending in which the client felt unheard and might have left in anger and disappointment could be turned into an ending with hope and possibility for the future.

The therapist's own ending

One of the main areas of difficulty in ending faced by all therapists is the matter of their own endings as therapists. Retirement is a word that has entirely different connotations depending on the position of the speaker. A man sweats away for a removal firm, trying to manoeuvre a piano up the stairs to a second floor flat. He has climbed the stairs innumerable times already. Yesterday, he emptied a house. Today, he fills one. Tomorrow and the day after, he will empty and fill others. He dreams of retirement, sitting in his chair in front of a football match on the television or taking the dog for a walk. Retirement is a long way off because he is still only in his forties, but he will have to go on doing this work for as long as he can manage it because he is not qualified for anything else. If his back starts to cause him trouble and he is lucky, he will be allowed a period of sitting at home, but it is possible that sooner or later he will be laid off to join the ranks of the unemployed. Honourable retirement at fifty or so would be a wonderful achievement for him.

At the other end of the spectrum is the therapist who trains at about the age of forty-five. This woman is getting into her stride at sixty-five. She has a number of long-term patients who are at various stages in the therapeutic process. She is gaining in experience and confidence in the essentials of the profession. She enjoys the continuing professional development meetings with colleagues and has ideas for writing a paper for a professional journal. This woman does not want to retire. She sees the potential lack of structure in her days, if she retires, as a drawback not an advantage. If she does not have to get up to see a patient at 8 am, why will she get up at all? Then she talks to her colleagues and decides that she must make plans to retire because it is unfair to her patients to go on until she becomes ill or incompetent or dies. Her hopes are quite different from those of the man who does physical work. The following extracts from interviews with therapists indicate the kind of hopes that might sustain an intelligent person with hopes for retiring:

Therapist A: I imagined, with a feeling of confidence, that I would do a whole variety of things that interest me, from spiritual direction to prison visiting, from hearing little children read to doing a great deal of walking, from visiting art galleries to seeing much more of family and longstanding friends.

Therapist B: Short answer - I don't see myself as a "retired therapist". I have had other work previously and do not see myself as a retired negotiator either. I feel free and able to do what I please with my life and time. My cello, playing music, studying subjects I had missed out on – I am on a course at City Lit this term on the influence of ancient Greek culture on surrounding cultures. Next term I will find another subject.

Therapist C: Generally I hope to feel "lighter" and less anxious and I hope to get to know my partner in a new way as we come face to face with new roles in life. I hope to make the most of life while we are still reasonably fit. I do not want to look back with too much regret because I lacked the courage to engage in new ways of being. I do expect to come across the same group of difficulties I have always experienced and feel more concerned about that than about lack of money or a prestigious role.

These three therapists have a positive attitude to the future and are able to visualise themselves in a new context with more time and with a sense of enjoyment. In order to hold this attitude, the mourning of the loss of the psychotherapist status has to take place. Therapist B above has already left the image of herself as a psychotherapist behind. She has apparently been able to mourn and to move out from the shadow of the object. The mourning process is an essential element to the success of a process of retirement. Therapists are aware that it is a process that must take place for their patients, and that they are unable to help because, by definition, they will not be there. This is one of the reasons why it is likely to be an achievement when a patient leaves and does not return. The difficulty for the therapist is that she will never know whether this silence is an indication of health and a movement through the process, or whether it is the result of the return of depression.

Working with depression

When she retires, the therapist will have an opportunity to observe her own ability to manage what she has needed to require of her patients. The psychoanalytic therapist has Freud's paper on "Mourning and melancholia" (Freud, 1917b) as a guide. This paper reveals an important stage in Freud's thinking, in which he was developing the ideas about the power of identification that he had begun in the paper on narcissism in 1914. James Strachey points out in his introduction that one of the most important ideas in this paper is that depression derives its power through the process by which an identification replaces an object cathexis. *Cathexis* was the word chosen by Strachey to translate the word *Besetzung* as used by Freud. Freud himself once used the antithesis "interest". In the present context, the patient identifies with a lost and helpless dead object instead of loving this object from the outside. Freud writes at length of the characteristics of depression and how we can see that they are like the conditions of mourning, and not like ordinary self-denigration. The person who feels shame wishes to hide it from others. The melancholic loses no opportunity to tell others how he feels. This is immediately understandable, Freud says, when we recognise that the reproaches are against someone else, not the patient at all. Does this have any relevance in the processes of ending and retirement?

Therapists will have seen some men and women who are suffering from the loss of a job or profession. These people do not frequently come to a therapist. For one thing, they often have too little money, but even more frequently they are convinced that they are not in need of any help. They just have to "get on with it" and accept the way things are. Those who do come, however, are sometimes suffering from melancholia or depression that can be related to an incomplete mourning process:

> Then the shadow of the object fell upon the ego and the latter could be judged henceforth by a special agency as though it were an object, the forsaken object. In this way an object loss was transformed into an ego loss. (Freud, 1917b, p. 249)

This beautifully turned passage sums up the result of our observations. The good may seem to be left behind with the lost way of life. The very existence of hope may make the experience of the loss better or worse, but does not seem to lead inevitably to a better experience after the loss. Freud points out that the one necessity is that there should have been a strong cathexis of the lost object. If the object is a person's working life, there will probably have been a strong cathexis either positive or negative.

The idea that the depressed person has identified his own ego with the lost object needs some additional thought when the loss is of a way of life rather than a person. Freud goes on to consider suicide, and the extent to which the ego has been able to take itself as an object and express its hatred and anger through self-murder:

> The analysis of melancholia now shows that the ego can kill itself only if owing to the return of the object cathexis it can treat itself as an object – if it is able to direct against itself the hostility which relates to an object and which represents the ego's original reaction to objects in the external world. (Ibid, p. 232)

This indicates that when working with a depressed patient, the therapist needs to try to track down the external object which has become the recipient of the patient's anger. For example, the patient who has retired unwillingly may blame a boss who, he thinks, had the authority to allow him to go on working a bit longer but did not. If that is not a viable fantasy, the patient may harbour angry feelings towards the Prime Minister or someone else who can be blamed for setting retirement age. This will be tenuous and the patient may be ashamed for harbouring strong views about this. Some people cannot find ways of pushing the anger outside themselves at all. One of the worst forms of melancholia is when the patient with some obsessional tendencies perhaps begins to feel that he has caused the loss himself. The therapist will have difficulties when the choice seems to be between depressive self-accusation and the paranoid blaming of others. Neither of these states of mind is comfortable. The transfer of the anger to the patient's own self will be easier if the alternative is not easily acceptable. The therapist will need to show understanding and empathy with the need to be able to feel and express anger about the situation, however unreasonable this might seem to the patient's ego.

Suicide

Suicide is a cause for anxiety among therapists. Each therapist knows or can imagine how painful it would be to lose a patient in this way. It is an ending to dread, even when the patient's position appears hopeless. There is no way in which the therapist can know for certain that it is hopeless. We are all unable to know the future, whether that involves new cures for physical illness or unexpected changes in mental states. Fortunately, we cannot know for certain that these things are impossible. This leads to two possible directions for the therapist. On the one hand, she may feel that she is wasting the patient's time and may wish to put an end to the therapy. She will be glad if the patient ends the therapy but I have never known a therapist who was able to agree that suicide would be the only option. The other direction of thinking is that the patient may get better, given a bit more time. The therapy will achieve improvements; it just has not done so yet.

This latter kind of hope is very difficult to assess. Conscientious therapists are bound to feel this way at times and it is very important that they should. Hope should not be erected simply to satisfy the narcissistic need to be successful. On the other hand, we have the example of Donald Winnicott. Harry Guntrip wrote a comparison of his two analyses with Fairbairn and Winnicott and shows how willing Winnicott was to accept that he might benefit from his patient's wisdom. (Guntrip, 1996, p. 737) Fairbairn was willing to accept that Guntrip had some insights and could add to, or even change, the conclusions that Fairbairn had already reached. Both of these analysts were able and willing to show the humility of the search for the truth, as best we can ever know it.

Saying to the patient that we do not have the answer or even that the future is unknown is often a difficult matter. It requires a sense of timing and an understanding of each individual that a clinician like Winnicott could manage, but which is difficult for most ordinary therapists. Yet the evidence is that patients can sometimes appreciate the honesty of "It's very hard for either of us to see how things can improve." This is a kind of honesty that can help the patient to consider what their options are, and perhaps to find some reserves of strength to make changes. The therapist has the duty to distinguish hope that is genuinely for the patient, from hope that is more for narcissistic satisfaction.

In the case of a suicidal patient, the therapist can face very great difficulties, both seeing and feeling the patient's hopelessness and also needing to stay on the side of life and hope. Unfortunately, the patient who is contemplating a serious suicide attempt is not likely to find that he can allow much hope in the therapist:

> Mr A was a seriously depressed patient who refused to take medication. He was seeing an inexperienced therapist, Ms P, who took him on in spite of seeing how depressed he was. He had left his job and had no interest in his family. He described his wife as "hopeless really". He went on: "She tries to understand but she has never been capable of seeing what bothers me. She is happy as long as she can get her nails done. She keeps food on the table, so the children are all right." The therapist was flattered by the implication that she was more capable of understanding him than his wife had been. She hoped that being able to talk through his feelings would free him to move away from his depression. She did not work out what might lie beneath his impatience with his wife. As a result, he grew angrier but presented a willingness to talk to Ms P. Although he

talked about how hopeless he felt and how little point there was in his continuing to exist, Ms P continued to feel hopeful and to say things like "I will hold the hope for you".

After some weeks, Mr A drowned himself in a gravel pit by weighting his pockets with stones. His therapist was informed in an e-mail by Mr A's wife. She said that she did not blame the therapist but thought that she should know. Ms P was shocked and profoundly ashamed when she heard this. She also felt extremely angry, although she tried to hide this from herself. She was not sure where the anger belonged but decided to consult with a senior member of the profession. Between them, they came to the conclusion that Mr A had been very angry. His wife was the main person hurt by Mr A's suicide, but there were also the people who found his car and had to drag the body from the water. His children were small, but they were already suffering from his absence and from his wife's distress.

Suicide is nearly always an expression of anger. It can hurt many people. Ms P had to live with not knowing whether it would have made any difference if she had dealt more effectively with his anger, but she did see that her rather complacent comments about hope might have increased the anger. He might have begun to see her as being, like his wife, more interested in doing her nails than in paying attention to his despair. This is very understandable. Can anyone understand despair without feeling it? The answer is probably not, but the attempt to understand it can be, perhaps,conveyed.

This story is fortunately not representative but does illustrate the importance of putting hope into a context where it can be useful, but not where it can be seen as the easy option for the therapist.

The next chapter will look at the difficulties caused by hope when the hope is not realised.

CHAPTER EIGHT

Was there a choice?

This book has considered some of the ways in which the mental state of the therapist interacts with that of the patient to lead to an ending which might not represent the ideal of either. The reasons why a particular ending might offend the superego of the therapist are varied, but coincide to some extent with the goals of the particular school of theory to which she subscribes. Since the theory described in this book has been confined to the analytic schools of therapy, this conclusion will look only at the reasons why an analytic therapist might look back with regret at an ending that took place. The general field in which the analytic therapist is working will be next to others but will have its own characteristics. For example, the Jungian will hope for integration of the shadow and the use of the transcendent function to enable the opposites to co-exist without causing illness. The Kleinian might hope for the use of the depressive position to predominate, and to be remembered even when the paranoid schizoid position is inhabited. The manic defences would be less important and the possibilities of reparation would be used. Contemporary

119

Freudians might be looking for genital maturity and the possibilities of constantly seeking to make the unconscious conscious. Jungians might also hope to see the patient acknowledging the darker side of himself that he does not like, and finding a way to allow opposites to co-exist. The therapist who has been trained to have a pluralist approach will consider all these aspects of readiness to end, and will have to suffer from knowing that they are not all met in any given case.

Given that it is true that for most therapists, the patient will leave without having achieved as much as she might have wished, she will have to recognise and manage her own guilt and disappointment. Consider the case of Emilia:

> Emilia was a woman in her late sixties who came to see a therapist, Jean. She was unsure about what exactly her problem was but she said she was very unhappy and cried a great deal. Her mother had died about six months before, and although Emilia was married and had a husband whom she described as "supportive but busy", she seemed isolated. The death of her mother was the subject that she brought to all her early sessions. She felt guilty and since the bereavement was not long ago, Jean was not surprised that the guilt of the survivor was still active. She heard the story and began to think that there was more to it than that. Emilia described her mother as an intelligent woman who was widowed in her early seventies. It was already noticeable that this was the description given, not that Emilia had lost her father. The mother's grief was understandably great and continued over many years. She lived in a house not far from the town in which Emilia lived, and it was therefore possible for Emilia to spend at least one mealtime a week with her. She also took her mother shopping and spent time with her there. As her mother aged, Emilia began to worry about her living alone. The people of the village in which she lived were friendly, but as her mother often said "not like having your own family nearby."

> As her mother more and more frequently spoke of being lonely and isolated, Emilia began to think about the possibility of moving her to sheltered housing in the town where she lived. At one point, a small flat in a sheltered housing project became available and she suggested to her mother that she might prefer to live there within easy reach of neighbours and friends who lived in the town. Her

mother agreed with some enthusiasm and Emilia said that she now thinks that this was because she expected to be nearer to Emilia, and therefore that there would be more time when she could be with her. The move was completed and her mother was established in the small flat. For about two years, this worked well in that it was possible to make friends and to enjoy a renewed social life in the friendly environment of the people who were mostly considerably younger, just in their sixties and seventies. The time came, however, when the mother suffered a fall and broke a leg. She was frail already and in a heavy plaster and was completely helpless. Emilia responded by talking to social services and asking whether someone could come and look after her mother at home; the answer was that this was not possible and she could enter a care home for respite care until her leg was better.

The place in a care home was arranged and the mother, who by this time was confused and suffering some disorientation from the pain killers that she was given, was moved into the care home by Emilia and her husband. At this point Emilia began to cry. "I knew I was doing a terrible thing to her. I knew she would hate it there but I was working and my sister in Australia could not help, although she was always willing to speak on the phone. We agreed that she could not be expected to go back home as she was already in her late eighties. Without discussing it with my mother at all we agreed that she should stay in the care home. This meant that we had to sell her house in order to pay the fees. She just stayed in the same room and never went home again. One friend who went to see her a few times told me that she would not complain but just said sadly, 'Emilia has decided that this will be the best thing for me.' I feel terrible. How could I do that to her?" Jean said: "I think it was time that did that to her. You responded to the circumstances, it seems to me."

Emilia was relieved by her therapist's attitude but it took many weeks of working through this grief and guilt for the feelings to abate a little. Her mother had died feeling more alone than ever in the care home, and the aim of keeping her safe seemed to have achieved something that she did not want and could not enjoy. She began to say that she wished she could die in her sleep and not wake up to another day. Emilia repeated her assurances that she wanted her mother to stay alive but her mind was no longer able to retain what was said to her for any length of time.

This case illustrates the pain of one who feels she has put an end to something and, in doing so, has done some damage—as in Emilia's case when she believed that she had destroyed her mother's happiness. The idea that age and time were to blame was some comfort, but the guilt needed much time to be considered and assuaged.

This sort of anxiety and guilt is experienced at times by therapists, although rarely in the full, painful form that derives from the memory of the mother and the child. Searles considered the patient as the Oedipal love object of the therapist in terms of the love from a parent to a child. (Searles, 1965) The pain of the child who must hurt the parent is a different, but perhaps equally painful, experience. This is most likely to be encountered with older patients and their parents, but is also possible when the patient is younger in years or experience. Both Emilia and her therapist were responding to the combination of the helplessness of the patient who had reached her eighties or nineties and had a physical and mental impairment, with the fact that she was the mother of the patient. The therapist also had a mother, and she too felt some of the guilt of the young at observing the deterioration of the once all-powerful, active mother into the pathetic figure of the old woman. Of course it had become necessary to look after her, but Emilia's guilt was not only bound up with remaining healthy and being younger, but also with her own fear of death and helplessness. She felt guilt for the unacknowledged wish to distance herself from the suffering of the old woman. After some time, she admitted to the therapist that her mother had wished to come and live with her even though Emilia and her husband were out at work all day. She had of course refused on the grounds that her mother would not be safe and also that she might be even lonelier. The mother never accepted this, always saying that she would prefer living with Emilia, whatever that meant, to living with strangers. Emilia had never acknowledged to herself that she did not want her mother in her house. She did not want to live with her mother's grief and loss at such close quarters and greatly valued the possibility of coming home from visiting her. This element was the kernel of the guilt which needed to be analysed before it could be left behind and replaced with sadness.

Some people consulting therapists have suffered similar dilemmas and have arrived at various solutions, most of which have left a residue of guilt. The reasons for the guilt can be pulling in opposite directions. On the one hand, there may be guilt for refusing what the parent wanted; on the other, there may be guilt for agreeing to it and then feeling resentment. First of all it will be useful to consider the situation of the therapist who has to terminate a therapy of an older person. Freud's argument that the sons would have a to wish to kill the father and remove the rival, needs to be developed for the woman who is forced to deny her mother the only gift that she wants; the return of her own youth, health and strength. Many old people do suffer a fall and there are all sorts of reasons for this, but young people want to blame them: "He was not wearing his emergency button." Or: "I told her that she needed to be careful of that step." Blame of course is for different things, but perhaps at its root is the anger with the parent for growing old and showing so clearly the likely fate of each one of us. Like the fall of man in western culture, the fall of the old person symbolises the end of the satisfying, good life, and the beginning of dependence and physical vulnerability.

The patient who is being told to terminate therapy so that the therapist can retire or move to another town is presenting her with a similar example of helplessness, and is therefore also to be shunned. This shunning can take various forms but it may cause the unwillingness to hear the full extent of the patient's emotional reaction. While the envy discussed in the previous chapter is possible, the therapist may wish to blot out the unfortunate patient who has to be relegated to a place which is outside. There is some deep tribal memory of leaving the old people behind which seems to be activated when a therapist has to insist on an ending, just as Emilia felt she had to insist on moving her mother on to the next stage of helplessness and decline.

Endings in training

One of the examples of this kind of response may be remembered from the training situation. Each therapist has been on a training course and the reputable ones will have to fail some students. In other words, some aspiring therapists have to be told that they are not suitable for this profession and should go and use their different talents elsewhere. Of course it would be preferable to discover this before allowing them to begin, but assessment is not accurate enough either for training or for therapy itself to predict exactly who will benefit, and so we often decide to give a chance to someone who is doubtful. Training courses are very reluctant to terminate training because they are aware of how much time, effort, and money can be invested by the candidate, and because it is so difficult to be sure in many of these situations. The people making the decisions are of course thera-pists themselves, and the guilt over the action that must be taken will be partly at least in the area of damage to the one who becomes weak and helpless. The way that the training course deals with people in this position will contribute to the formation of the therapists who will have to say no to their own clients in different ways. The termi-nation of training is a process which most therapists can remember if it happened to a colleague while they were in the training.

Angela was a trainee on the first year of a training course. Her background was in business where she had worked as an adminis-trator. At one point she had been asked to act as a temporary recep-tionist and had needed to talk to the general public who passed by her. She had developed a skill in cheerful, casual talk and could usually get people to talk to her while they waited for their ap-pointment. Her colleagues told her she was a good listener and she should be a counsellor. She thought that sounded good and she would like to help people. The counselling training course to which she applied carried out interviews, but relied on the first year to weed out those who were unsuitable. The interviewer did say to her that professional counselling was very different from chatting to people, but decided to give her a chance. She did not pay much attention to what she was told and began the course full of confi-dence and anticipation. During the first year, there were many role playing exercises in which Angela was the client or the counsellor. She found that she could be either with equal enthusiasm. In fact, she enjoyed being the counsellor where she could give the client good advice. She learnt that giving advice was not the role of the counsellor but said "it just seemed so obvious that I couldn't help saying it." Her teachers worried about this tendency, but blamed themselves for not having made it clear enough to Angela the rea-sons for not giving advice. Angela was given a viva in order to pass that year and move on to clinical work. She was asked about the reasons for not giving advice and said blithely "Well it isn't analysing I suppose". This was seen as a good enough answer and she was allowed to pass.

Trouble began in earnest when she started seeing clients. Her supervisor, Mrs P, was satisfied with the way she began work and made a good enough relationship with the client for the work to begin. There was no apparent problem until her new client left without comment after three sessions. Angela was puzzled. "I can't see why she would have left. I did tell her that she should think about leaving her partner. He is not good for her and I told her so." "You didn't tell me that you said that", said the supervisor, somewhat shocked. "Oh didn't I?" said Angela, innocently. "I must have forgotten. It was right at the end of the session." The supervisor noted this but let it go, until something similar happened with the next client. The work seemed to begin well, but after only five sessions the same thing happened. The client left and Angela said she had no idea why. "I can't see why she wouldn't stay as she still has problems at work. Of course she would have been better getting another job as I told her but if she persisted in staying there, at least she might have been more able to say what she found so difficult and then negotiated changes with her manager." The supervisor could see the sense of this, but still pointed out that this was based on an instruction which the client was well able to ignore in order, perhaps, to have a small triumph over one kind of manager. Angela did not see this at all. "I wasn't telling her to do anything; I was just stating the alternatives for her." Mrs P was not very happy with this but hoped that it had indeed been a summary of what the client had actually said herself. She said this and Angela seemed happy. "Yes, of course", she said.

The case of Angela shows how difficult the role of a supervisor can be. She does not know the detail or even the degree of accuracy of what she is being told. She has to take the account of the sessions on trust. The only way she can tell that she might not be hearing the whole story is when she hears different accounts of the same occasion, or when, as with Angela, she is told fragments of what must have been a bigger picture.

Mrs P began to worry about Angela, with a growing conviction that she did not accept the most basic tenets of analytic work. She seemed to think that her role was to improve the lives of her clients, not just to help them understand themselves so that they could make their own improvements more successfully. Mrs P suggested to the Training Committee that they should offer an interview to Angela so that they could judge for themselves whether or not she was fit to practise and should be allowed to move into the psychoanalytic psychotherapy training. The Committee decided to do this, as the supervisor was not able to give an unequivocal recommendation that Angela could qualify. Angela, of course, asked her supervisor what the problem was as most people were simply sent a letter saying that they could move on. The supervisor told her honestly what her problem was and why she was worried. Angela listened and said she understood.

At her viva, Angela was asked why she would not give advice to a client. She answered in more or less the words of her supervisor. She also said, "I know I made a bit of a mistake with one client but I have seen what I did wrong and of course I will not make the same mistake again." The Committee considered what she had said and agreed that they had enough to think that she would probably qualify. Then one member of the Committee, Dr Jones, spoke up and said, "I am not happy with this. I think we should ask the supervisor to come and speak with us. This is an unusual case and we are putting future clients at risk if we let her go." The others were irritated that they could not conclude the case there and then, but reluctantly agreed that there was an ethical question that should be resolved.

Angela's supervisor was surprised to be asked to attend a special committee meeting. There was no precedent that she knew about, but she could see that suggesting a viva also had no precedent and she would have to do her best to be fair and make the system work. She spent considerable time thinking about Angela's work, and she realised that she did not have any grounds for encouragement. She asked herself what she could say about the criteria for qualification. How far could she say that Angela met them? She found that she had no positive evidence and the evidence that she had was all negative. She realised that she could not recommend that Angela should continue in the training. Most obviously, she was afraid that Angela remained unconvinced that she should not give advice, and was likely to do it again.

On the other hand, recommending that she should leave would cause a great deal of commotion among the other people in her year. She would have to carry the burden of being the bad person. The big question was: could she defend her position if she needed to? Mrs P found herself already planning this, and decided that she must have accepted that this was the plan she must follow. She told the committee that it was difficult to support this graduation, and she had thought about whether she would be willing to refer people to Angela if she was allowed to qualify. She had come to the conclusion that she would not. The committee asked for some more detail about the work that was brought for supervision. She told them about one of the cases that had terminated, and one that continued for several months which was the longest that for which clients had attended. Dr Jones listened attentively and shook her head. "I am not convinced that we can pass her with any honour or honesty." The Training committee voted and then unanimously agreed that Angela should be failed and should be told that she needed to find an alternative profession. Perhaps she could go back to working in the City and could use her skills in befriending people.

Mrs P was sent a letter saying that, as a result of her helpful information and the reports received, Angela was to terminate her training. Two weeks later, she received another letter saying that Angela had submitted an appeal against the conclusion of the committee. The grounds given were that Mrs P had not treated her fairly. She had written that from the beginning she had felt that Mrs P was prejudiced against her. The Committee thought that this was a serious accusation and they would need to investigate. Mrs P was shocked and extremely worried. She was puzzled about how she could prove a negative. That led to the thought that perhaps the Committee would require proper evidence from Angela which, of course, she would not be able to provide. She did worry that everything that happened had been between two individuals in private. The result was that any hearing would have to decide which of the two was more credible. In fact, the Committee held the hearing and decided that there was no evidence that Mrs P had treated her unfairly. Angela's training was terminated. To begin with, Mrs P was just relieved but gradually she began to worry. She had found herself being angry and resentful and very much wanting Angela to be sent away. This led to some guilt and anxiety that it might have been the wrong decision. After all, Angela had been at the very beginning of her training and she might have learned to see her role as the rest of the profession did. On the other hand, one of the most important qualities of a psychotherapist is the willing-ness to learn and Angela had not demonstrated that.

Termination of training analysis is complicated by the training situa-tion and the post analytic relationship. The candidate may not feel free to terminate. Abandoning a therapist who has been important in giving support, and who has been a teacher that has shown the can-didate how to manage the difficulties of a life in training, may be prevented partly by the sense of gratitude. Training therapy may feel like a gift. Gifts bring obligation which may add to the genuine hu-man gratitude. Patients who have spent many years in training will be able to understand the feelings of the therapist, and will perhaps be torn between the feeling of gratitude and the ability to assert their own need.

The therapist may be very attached to a candidate who has gone through all the vicissitudes of training, and this alone may make it difficult to accept the need for termination. At the same time, there may be prestige in having a number of candidates in training, and the therapist may be loath to see the ending of the relationship. If the candidate chooses to end immediately after he is qualified, this may feel to the therapist like a confirmation that he has attended his therapy so far only because it was required, and the same may be true for the training analyst. The candidate and his own patient may terminate simultaneously, and analyses will generally be burdened by multiple terminations.

> Termination is particularly painful for the analyst if he has very few analysands and is faced with not fulfilling his analytic goals and ideals. In addition, with insufficient analytic practice, the ana-lyst will not be eligible to become a training analyst. Training may not be truly terminated until the analyst becomes a training ana-lyst in his own right, equal with his own analyst (unconsciously, a parent-analyst with his own child-candidate). (Blum, 1989)

Since all of this affects the therapist's wish to maintain a training therapy, the few occasions in which the therapist starts to worry about the fitness of her patient to practise psychotherapy are particularly painful. In the case of Angela, Mrs P, the supervisor, might well have hoped that the training therapist, Dr Y, would have understood the problem and might have been able to tackle it. The therapist, on the other hand, who heard more about the supervisor, was in fact very concerned about the grounds given for appeal.

The therapist's role

The therapist had heard nothing to suggest that there had been any unfair treatment until the Training Committee began to consider its conclusion. On the other hand, she had noted that Angela had a very inflated view of her own ability. What the interviewers for the training course had heard about as a conviction that she was a good listener, came across to her therapist as a sense of entitlement which seemed to indicate the grandiosity of a narcissistic personality. She hoped that she would be able to make interpretations which would enable Angela to think about her view of other people. When the therapist said, "Do you think your supervisor might have had a good reason for what she said?" Angela lost her temper and stormed out saying, "You are on her side. You are not thinking about me at all." This focus on the self began to worry Dr Y. How was she going to be able to think with generosity and empathy about her patients if she could not even bear to think about such a question? How much love had she ever received if she could not see a question like this as having some use, coming from someone who had shown patience and care for her already? The appeal against the training committee decision was the final indication that there was no change.

Dr Y began to consider whether she had an ethical duty to inform the Training Committee of her fears. She was very reluctant to do so and conducted an argument with herself about it for some time. She consulted a senior member of the profession in strict confidence about her concerns, and received support to try to go on and make a difference. "Leave it to the supervisor" was the advice. "You will do more good by staying with her. If you report her you will lose her for sure." Reassured, she continued to see the patient who left when her training was terminated. This disturbed Dr Y. The patient showed no interest in understanding her own part in the events. She was full of anger and righteous indignation against the supervisor and the Training Committee. This led Dr Y to feel some guilt. She should have reported her doubts about Angela to the Training Committee, and yet there was still the argument that it was not her job and she should concentrate on her analytic task. Her consultant told her that she had done the best she could and yet Dr Y still had some doubt: "Is there ever a good enough reason to report someone who is training?" "I think so. I think that if you have serious ethical concerns and to the best of your knowledge the supervisors are not seeing the same thing, then you probably will have to say something, telling the patient that you are going to do it. There would need to be a period in which you give the patient an opportunity to understand your concerns and see whether she can make some use of them. That would take empathy and skill but therapists ought to be prepared to do it if they are going to take on candidates in training."

So far, this chapter has considered the difficult decisions made by therapists when training questions arise. The trainees also have to make the decision to stay and complete the course in spite of their fears and often debilitating anxiety. Anyone who works in a university counselling service will be familiar with the profound anxiety of many students in their first term. They will see others who seem confident and self-assured. They will be away from home, in some cases for the first time, and this will lead to loneliness and a tendency to withdraw and stay in their room, too nervous to make friends or even work effectively. The adult who takes on a training course in adult years has different problems, but no less severe in some cases. The adult coming from a pre-existing career knows that he is successful enough in that field but is faced with a completely different approach and set of ethical and professional standards. Even worse for the adult student is the requirement to write essays and papers. The person with a PhD in History or Philosophy might feel deeply ashamed by difficulties in writing an essay in this new subject with new criteria and norms. This might lead to problems in being open to learning, which by definition requires a certain amount of humility. Only the student who is prepared to be a student, and acknowledge that she needs to learn, will have much hope of success.

The consequence of this may be that some people consider dropping out. The new undergraduates in their first term have a high drop-out rate, and in fact a high rate of failure. Some are so disturbed that they attempt or carry out suicide. Candidates for psychotherapy training generally do not have a high suicide rate, and we might think that the requirement for personal therapy helps them to survive. On the other hand, some do drop out. This might be the best decision as it might be helpful for them to choose to leave before they are required to do so. The choice is a difficult one, but the role playing that is involved in most early years of training courses helps people to understand the demands on the therapist and the need to listen intently and think quickly. It also teaches the need for restraint and, as in the case of Angela, the need to deny oneself the satisfaction of giving advice. On the other hand, the role playing situation requires a certain amount of acting ability. The person who finds this difficult may not always see its relevance in helping people to understand the working of their own minds, but may discover a great deal that is disturbing about his or her own wishes and demands. This may be too much to take, and may be so upsetting that the candidate realises that she cannot continue with the process. If this is so, leaving at this point will be much the wisest thing to do.

Retirement

Among the most difficult endings for the therapist is the process of his or her own ending in retirement. The therapist's feelings about this have been considered in Chapter Six. Unless the therapist dies while still working, all therapists will have to plan and carry out a process of retirement, and will have to do it responsibly for the good of their patients. An example of how this can affect patients is the suicide of the psychoanalyst, Nina Coltart. She had written a number of accessible books which were well known to therapists, and to some of their patients as well. Her suicide was a puzzle, at least to those who did not know her well. Her decision to move on from this life seemed to send messages conveying that even the best analysed and most thoughtful among us might not be able to make life worth continuing to live. Once the process of therapy or analysis is complete, the therapist has to make the best of her life for her own sake and still partly for the sake of the patients, who will hear about what she does in some cases and will either suffer or benefit from the knowledge. Of the nine retired therapists who have been interviewed, five were happy or very happy with their new state, while four were still unsure that the new life they were living was worthwhile.

Comments fall into such areas as the need to feel useful, and the difficulty of finding voluntary work that makes use of the particular skills of the ex-therapist. Two therapists mentioned the difficulty of finding a satisfactory new identity. One mentioned the fear that no-one would be interested in "I used to be a ..." as opposed to "I am a ..." Moving to a new city meant that none of the people she met knew the role that she once had filled and treated her as an old lady, but with none of the respect to which she had been accustomed in her working life. One person had many interests, and a sense that there was still much to be discovered and enjoyed. One was enjoying time to play the cello. One was disappointed to find that travelling was already too much of an effort and too difficult, even though that had been one of the reasons for seeking to retire at sixty-eight rather than leaving it until later. Those who had been retired for a year or more were more satisfied with their lives than those who had just entered the state. This is a small sample and it would be helpful to know whether that is still the case with a larger group.

Although some therapists regret their retirement and look back with sadness and nostalgia at the days when they were working, it is difficult for them, as for any group of retired people, to distinguish the loss of the professional role from the loss of youth and vigour. Both are important losses, but the loss of youth is one that must just be accepted. The loss of the professional role can be accepted with equanimity as some of our therapists have already shown us. For both losses, there are consolations if they can be allowed to show themselves. Most of those who had retired, especially the most recently retired, mentioned the relief of not having to worry about their patients, especially the worry about daily routines such as getting up early and being ready and available at the appropriate time. Freedom and being able to do what you like at any time of day is something that can be enjoyed only when the therapist is able to leave behind her own guilt about no longer working. The self-indulgence of being able to choose how to fill one's day by one's own choice needs to be specifically allowed by the superego. It may need some work on each person's own past, particularly the guilt towards the parents who are often visualised as working hard and, in some cases, being disappointed. The child with these images of disappointed parents finds it difficult to allow herself the luxury of not working.

The idea of work is complex in our society in the twenty-first century. The definition is generally "activity that involves effort". This means that the guilt is likely to relate to the effort involved. There is more to it than just effort because patients and ex-therapists too need convincing that keeping a house, cooking, gardening, etc. is work, and enough to enable an individual to feel that she is contributing to her friends, relatives, and community. The idea of what work is may need to change when a person retires. She may have gone along with the general belief that work is something that you go to and spend seven hours or so doing so that you can feel entitled to enjoy leisure. A retired person needs to redefine work so that she is able to enjoy leisure and distinguish it from effortful activity. Since we spend a good deal of time working on the management of guilt, we are obliged to show some competence in dealing with it in our own lives. It seems appropriate to end where we began in this cyclical process, but with the hope that the process of reading these thoughts will have made a difference. Endings of all sorts, not just in death, are starkly envisaged by Philip Larkin.

Most things will not happen. This one will. (Larkin, 2003)

We know that death and endings will happen, and we owe it to our patients to face that truth and make it as good as it can be.

REFERENCES

Barnes, J. (2008). *Nothing to be Frightened of.* London: Jonathan Cape.

Barzilai, S. (1997). "History is not the Past": Lacan's critique of Ferenczi. *Psychoanalytic Review, 84:* 553–572.

Bion, W. R. (1967). Notes on memory and desire. *Psychoanalytic Forum, 2:* 271–280.

Bion, W. R. (1970). *Attention and Interpretation.* London: Tavistock.

Blake, W. (1794). The Poison Tree. In: A. Ostriker (Ed.), *The Complete Poems of William Blake.* Harmondsworth: Penguin Poets, 1977.

Blanco, M. (1988). *Thinking, Feeling and Being.* London: Routledge.

Blum, H. (1989). The concept of termination and the evolution of psychoanalytic thought. *Journal of the American Psychoanalytic Association, 37:* 275–295.

Blume-Marcovici, A., Stolberg, R., & Khademi, M. (2013). Do therapists cry in therapy? The role of experience and other factors in therapists' tears. *Psychotherapy.* DOI: 10.1037/a0031384.

Breuer, J., & Freud, S. (1895). Studies on hysteria. *S.E., 2:* 3–17. London: Hogarth.

Castelnuovo-Tedesco, P. (1986). Fear of changes as a source of resistance in analysis. *Annual of Psychoanalysis, 14:* 259–272.

Coen, S. (2007). Narcissistic temptations to cross boundaries and how to manage them. *Journal of the American Psychoanalytic Association, 55:* 1169–1190.

Cooper, E., Hamilton, M., Gangure, D., & Roose, P. (2004). Premature termination from psychoanalysis: an investigation of factors contributing to early endings. *Journal of the American Psychoanalytic Association, 52*: 1233–1234.

Eliot, T. S. (1925). The Hollow Men. In: Eliot, T., *Collected Poems*. London: Faber and Faber, 1936.

Eliot, T. S. (1944). *Four Quartets*. London: Faber and Faber.

Erikson, E. (1965). *Childhood and Society*. Harmondsworth: Penguin.

Ferenczi, S. (1991). In: M. Stanton (Ed.), *Sandor Ferenczi: Reconsidering Active Intervention*. New York, NY: Jason Aronson Publishers, 1991.

Franklin, B. (1817). *Autobiography*. In: L. J. Lemay & P. Zall (Eds.), *Benjamin Franklin's Autobiography*. New York, NY: Norton Critical Editions, 1986.

Freud, S. (1900). In: J. Masson (Ed.), *The Complete Letters of Sigmund Freud to Wilhelm Fliess*. Cambridge, MA: Harvard University Press, 1985.

Freud, S. (1909b). Analysis of a phobia in a five year old boy. *S.E., 10*: 5–149. London: Hogarth.

Freud, S. (1909d). Notes upon a case of obsessional neurosis. *S.E., 10*: 152–249. London: Hogarth.

Freud, S. (1913). On beginning the treatment. *S.E., 12*: 123–144. London: Hogarth.

Freud, S. (1915). Thoughts for the times on war and death. *S.E., 14*: 273–300. London: Hogarth.

Freud, S. (1915). Observations on transference love. *S.E., 12*: 159–171. London: Hogarth.

Freud, S. (1916). On transience. *S.E., 14*: 305–307. London: Hogarth.

Freud, S. (1917). Mourning and melancholia. *S.E., 14*: 239–258. London: Hogarth.

Freud, S. (1925d). Inhibitions, symptoms and anxiety. *S.E., 20*: 77–172. London: Hogarth.

Freud, S. (1933a). New Introductory Lectures on Psycho-Analysis. *S.E., 22*: 3–182. London: Hogarth.

Freud, S. (1937a). Analysis terminable and interminable. *S.E. 23*: 211–23. London: Hogarth.

Frost, R. (1920). Fire and ice. In: R. Frost, *Selected Poems by Robert Frost*. Harmondsworth: Penguin Poets, 1962.

Gabbard, G. O. (1995). The early history of boundary violations in psychoanalysis. *Journal of the American Psychoanalytic Association, 43*: 1115–1136.

Gay, P. (1988). *Freud: A Life for Our Time*. London: Papermac.

Grosskurth, P. (1996). *Melanie Klein*. London: Hodder and Stoughton.

Guntrip, H. (1996). My experience of analysis with Fairbairn and Winnicott. International Journal of Psychoanalysis, 77: 239.

Heenan-Wolff, S. (2013). Translation and transformation in the analytic situation: Freud, Bion, Laplanche. *International Journal of Psychoanalysis*, *94*(3): 437–451.

Heimann, P. (1963). Joan Riviere (1883-1962). *International Journal of Psychoanalysis*, *44*: 228–235.

Hill, P. (2002). *Using Lacanian Clinical Technique*. London: Press for the Habilitation of Psychoanalysis.

Hurn, H. (1971). Towards a paradigm of the terminal phase: The current status of the terminal phase. *Journal of the American Psychoanalytic Association, 19*: 332–348.

Jacobs, M. (2005). *The Presenting Past*. London: International Universities Press.

Jung, C. G. (1954). *The Practice of Psychotherapy*. R.F.C. Hull (Trans). London: Routledge and Kegan Paul.

Kegerreis, S. (2013). When I can come on time I'll be ready to finish: meanings of lateness in psychoanalytic psychotherapy. *British Journal of Psychotherapy, 29*(4): 449–465.

Khan, M. (1973). The role of illusion in the analytic space and process. *Annals of Psychoanalysis, 1*: 231–246.

Klein, M. (1940). Mourning and its relation to manic depressive states. In: Klein, M., *Love, Guilt and Reparation*. London: Hogarth Press, 1985.

Klein, M. (1975). *Envy and Gratitude and other Works 1946–1963*. London: Hogarth Press and the Institute of Psycho-Analysis.

Kohut, H. (1971). *The Analysis of the Self*. New York, NY: International University Press.

Kohut, H. (1979). The two analyses of Mr Z. *International Journal of Psychoanalysis, 60*: 3–27.

Kung, H. (1979). *Freud and the Problem of God*. (Enl. 1990 ed.). New Haven, CT: Yale University Press.

Lacan, J. (1949). *Le Stade du Miroir Comme Formateur de la Fonction du Je*. Ecrits, Paris: Seuil. In: Lacan, J., *Ecrits à Selection*. A. Sheridan (Trans). London: Tavistock, 1977.

Lacan, J. (1964). *The Four Fundamental Concepts of Psychoanalysis*. A. Sheridan (Trans), London: Hogarth, 1979.

Laplanche, J., & Pontalis, J.-B. (1973). *The Language of Psychoanalysis*. D. Nicholson-Smith (Trans). London: Hogarth.

Larkin, P. (1977). Aubade. In: A. Thwaite (Ed.), *Philip Larkin: Collected*

Poems. London: Faber and Faber, 1988.

Levy, S., & Young, L. (2004). Difficulties with potency post trauma. In: S. Levy & S. Lemma (Eds.), *The Perversion of Loss* (pp. 127–144). London: Whurr.

Loftus, E. F., & Bernstein, D. M. (2002). Lingering difficulties distinguishing true from false memories: a comment on Shevrin's psychoanalytic view of memory. *Neuropsychoanalysis, 4*: 139–141.

Lowe, G. (1972). *The Growth of Personality*. Harmondsworth: Penguin.

McDougall, J. (1992). An interview. *Psychoanalytic Dialogues, 2*: 97–115.

Molnos, A. (1995). *A Question of Time*. London: Karnac.

Murdin, L. (1999). *How Much is Enough? Endings in Psychotherapy and Counselling*. London: Routledge.

Orbach, A. (1996). *Not Too Late*. London: Jessica Kingsley.

Pearson, J. (Ed.) (2004). *Analyst of the Imagination: The Life and Work of Charles Rycroft*. London: Karnac.

Rempel, M. (1997). Understanding Freud's philosophy of religion. *Canadian Journal of Psychoanalysis, 5*: 215–242.

Rycroft, C. (1955). Illusion and disillusion. *International Journal of Psychoanalysis, 36*: 81–87.

Samuels, A. (1989). *The Plural Psyche*. London: Routledge.

Searles, H. (1965). *Collected Papers on Schizophrenia*. London: Maresfield.

Segal, J. (2004). *Mélanie Klein*. London: Sage.

Shakespeare, W. (1606). *Macbeth*. In: *The Complete Works of William Shakespeare*. New York: Garden City, 1936.

Spence, D. (2003). Listening for rhetorical truth. *Psychoanalytic Quarterly, 72*: 875–903.

Turnbull, H.W. (Ed.) (1959). *The Correspondence of Isaac Newton. 1*: 416. Cambridge: CUP.

Winnicott, D. W. (1960). Ego distortion in terms of true and false self. In Winnicott, D. W., *The Maturational Processes and the Facilitating Environment* (pp. 140–152). London: Hogarth, 1965.

Winnicott, D. W. (1962). The aims of psychoanalytic treatment. In Winnicott, D. W., *The Maturational Processes and the Facilitating Environment* (pp. 166–170). London: Hogarth, 1965.

Winnicott, D. W. (1965). *The Maturational Processes and the Facilitating Environment*. London: Hogarth.

Winnicott, D. W. (1971). *Playing and Reality*. Harmondsworth: Penguin.

Winnicott, D. W. (1971). Transitional objects and transitional phenomena. In L. Caldwell & A. Joyce (Eds.), *Reading Winnicott*. London: Routledge, 2011.

Index